Time Zero

Center Stage---

Theater of the Universe!

© Mike Norton

**Silent stone sentinels testify to moments
in ancient history when tumultuous events etched
paths of change across earth's landscape.**

Cover
Rebecca Paschal's stunning cover design frames
Mike Norton's photo of a gnarled Bristlecone Pine, clinging to life
on the rocky slopes of California's Sierra Mountains.

Warren LeRoi Johns

Author of *Chasing Infinity, Genesis File, Beyond Forever,
Ride to Glory,* and *Dateline Sunday, U.S.A.*

Time Zero

© Jasper James

Publisher: www.GenesisFile.com
Printer: Lightning Source, LaVergne, Tennessee
ISBN: 978-0-615-44106-1

Library of Congress Control Number: 2011920916

Recognizing Greatness

"The great person, the great man,
is the miracle of history." *

John the Revelator authored the gospel of John based on
his eyewitness account of Christ's ministry, death and resurrection.
Living late in the first century A.D., John devoted his life preaching
Christianity and penning the Book of Revelation depicting
the church's perilous road to end-time victory.

Augustine (Aurelius Augustinus, 354-430), Bishop of Hippo,
influential Christian leader, writer, and theologian, is credited with
having played a pivotal role in merging the Old and New Testaments
in the *Holy Bible* canon during the Synod of Hippo, 393 A.D.

John Wycliffe (1328-1384), courageous fourteenth century scholar,
defied the religious establishment in 1382 by translating
the Bible into English to be accessible to the public.

Johannes Gutenberg (1398-1468), printing press pioneer,
published 180 copies of the original Latin Vulgate version
of the *Holy Bible* between the years 1450-1455.

* **Carl Sandburg's words recognized Abraham Lincoln as a** *"great person!"*
Time Zero **honors four others who championed God's truth**
and the miracle of His creation.

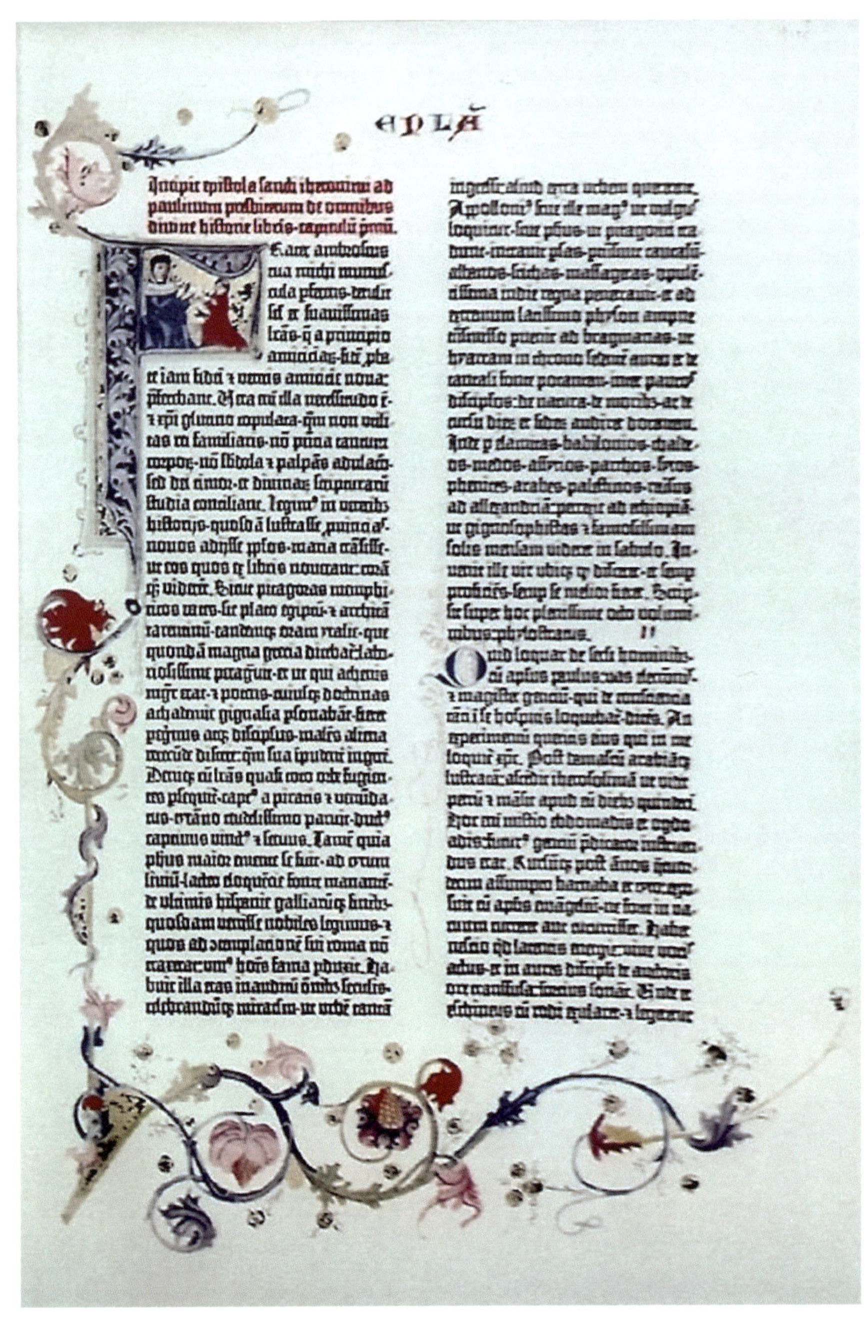

Johannes Gutenberg, pioneer book publisher,
printed one-hundred eighty copies of the *Gutenberg Bible*.
This Genesis One replica, complete with handcrafted illuminations,
is s reproduction taken from one of
the original surviving copies.

A Fresh Look at the Evidence

OZYMANDIAS [1]

I met a traveler from an antique land

Who said: Two vast and trunkless legs of stone

Stand in the desert.

Near them, on the sand,

Half sunk, a shattered visage lies, whose frown

And wrinkled lip, and sneer of cold command

Tell that its sculptor well those passions read

Which yet survive, stamped on these lifeless things,

The hand that mocked them and the heart that fed.

And on the pedestal these words appear:

"My name is Ozymandius, king of kings:

Look on my works, ye Mighty, and despair!"

Nothing beside remains.

Round the decay of that colossal wreck,

Boundless and bare

The lone and level sands stretch far away.

Percy Bysshe Shelley's *Ozymandius* captured the essence of human ego's thirst for power, inevitably confined to the limits of its finite dimension.

Penned by Shelley 41 years before Darwin published *Origin, Ozymandius* seems a fitting obituary for evolution's *"superstitious nonsense."* Deep within human thought is a sense there must be someone *"bigger than you and I."*

Evolution theory, bows its knee to dark philosophy leading to a forever death. Pagan cultures have worshiped the sun, fashioned idols from stone and crowned tyrannical monarchs as "gods." The infinite living, Lord God Almighty created all energy, matter and life. He alone is the one, true God, worthy of worship.

I

Playing the Time Card

Radiometric Dating

"Researchers have uncovered biological molecules like proteins, DNA, and pigments from rocks that are supposedly millions of years old…Many of these materials…will only survive thousands, not millions, of years." [1]

Brian Thomas

© visdia

Splitting the atom unleashes radioactive destructive power.
Unable to create an atom, technology has discovered radiometric
dating as a geochronological tool.

**Deep time represents the mother lode of evolution theory.
Without mega-millions of years, evolution conjecture
washes away like fool's gold in a mountain stream.**

More than 150 years after Darwin challenged the Genesis account of the origin of life on Planet Earth, his conjectures defy validation.

An "Intelligent Design" advocate, writing in, 2009, spotlighted some of the critical setbacks gnawing away at evolution's core fabric.

"In a year in which Darwin's disciples were celebrating the 200th anniversary of his birth that the 150th anniversary of the publication of On the Origin of Species, mainstream scientific journals published articles declaring: (1) the modern synthesis was dead, (2) Darwin's tree of life should be abandoned, (3) new "missing links" were a bust, (4) limits to Darwinism were demonstrated in the lab, (5) evolutionary icons like the peppered moths reverted back to their old colors, (6) the Cambrian Explosion lacks any plausible materialist explanation, and (7) an interdisciplinary revolution is occurring in biology that rejects the reductionist paradigm of Darwinian evolution." [2]

Life did not create itself by spontaneous generation. Even in a laboratory, human designers have been unable to create the simplest fully-functioning cell from non-living matter.

A living cell is more complex than any man-made mechanism.

The original source of DNA information mystifies.

Mutations typically degrade the genome rather than provide the *"raw material"* for natural selection to devise new and different life forms.

Stasis dominates the fossil record rather than millions of still-missing, transitional links.

Irreducible complexity of living systems defies evolution theory!

Charles Darwin's *"natural selection,"* purported to *"advance by short and sure, though slow, steps,"* requires multi-millions of years to work its transition myth up the ladder---from microbes to fish, to amphibians, to reptiles, to mammals, and ultimately to humans.

Ever since he first floated his ideas publicly in 1859, scientific evidence has been unkind to his conjecture. By tests he himself set up, the case for evolution hangs in limbo! Given Darwin's shaky house of cards, evolution theorists look the other way and play the time card.

Aided and abetted by a complicit media, multi-millions of years of deep time, has emerged as a strategy to skirt the yawning gaps in evolution's unproven postulate. Time calibration defines a cutting-edge issue, rising to lynchpin status in pre-history analysis. Geochronology represents an ideological touchstone!

Nineteenth-century evolutionists conjectured 25 million years as time enough for random chance gradualism to work evolution's wonders. This number has been overwritten by today's guesstimates.

Debunked, dismantled and disarticulated, evolution advocates try to squeeze the concept through an academic back door. Open-ended deep time is an imperative to support Darwin's prediction that *"all corporeal and mental endowments will tend to progress to perfection."* [3]

The daily miracle of live human births flies in the face of evolution theory. Darwin estimated a time lapse of millions of years before that first living cell, spawned accidentally from some *"warm little pond,"* would *"progress"* upward to achieve *Homo sapiens* status.

In the real world, it takes only nine months for a single sperm cell to unite with a single egg cell to produce a living, breathing human baby. In the several thousand years of recorded history, human reproduction has never shown the least hint of evolving a new and different life form at variance with the gene pool inherited from two human parents.

Even deep time may not be deep enough to salvage the legend of life's accidental origin and transitional development. The numbers game is anything but slam-dunk! Nor is it rocket science!

Screened by probability mathematics, the theory's *iffiness* collapses in a cloud of cosmic dust with or without deep time in play. Even 4.5 billion years is not enough time to ratify the imaginings of the Englishman. Evolution's deep time placebo is a mirage!

Evolution theory, evolving a full spectrum of plant and animal life forms, is less likely than six billion people solving a Rubik's Cube three-dimensional puzzle, simultaneously, in less than a minute.

Extremely improbable?

How about absolute impossibility!

As evolution's iconic gradualism theory crumbles, geochronology science has emerged to measure decay rates of inorganic elements. Ernest Rutherford introduced radiometric dating in 1905 as a methodology to determine the earth's age.

Facing assaults on a theory in jeopardy, die-hard evolutionists seized the new technology as a collateral challenge to the Genesis account of origins. The reasoning, "How could the Scripture narrative be true if radiometric dating produced multi-million year numbers?"

The answer was not slam-dunk!

For one thing, the date of death of a fossil residue of a once living organism does not necessarily take on the geochronological age of the burial site's inorganic matter.

For another, while the authoritative phrase, radiometric dating, can intimidate, it can be plagued also by nagging discordance or outside the range of reliable analysis. For example, *"The most crucial dates in modern human evolution are unfortunately beyond the range of the radiocarbon method…"* [4]

The ratio of ^{14}C to ^{12}C is used to date organic life systems. Measuring isotope ratios to determine age, has produced results that may expose the Achilles Heel of evolution's old-life scenario.

C-14 dating of fossilized life forms determines maximum ages---never *"older than their C-14 content would allow."* [5] The outer limit of C-14 dating is measured only in "thousands" rather than "millions" of years---a result not helpful to evolution theory.

Determining the C-14 to C-12 ratio to calibrate antiquity of a fossilized life form requires an accurate starting date. If the actual time of day is 6 A.M. but a clock is set erroneously at 12 midnight, the clock will never show the correct time however synchronously it ticks.

When a plant or animal dies, it no longer takes in C-14 but its C-12 remains constant. The comparative ratio of the two and the rate of decay is used conventionally as a reference tool for calculating the date of death.

In the event the C-14 in the atmosphere is increasing faster than it is decaying, the C-14 to C-12 ratio would require readjustment and the Carbon-14 time "clock" reset.

Even if the ratio remains constant and stable over time, the outside limits of the findings would be measured in only thousands and not millions of years!

"Carbon-14 is used to date dead plants and animals because plants and animals incorporate C-14 into their bodies by eating, drinking, and breathing in an environment containing C-14…

"When the organism dies, however, it ceaes to incorporate carbon into its body…Both C-14 and CC-14 to C-12 decreases slowly for thousands of years after the death of the organism." [5]

Coal seams, fossil residue from trees and vegetation buried deep in the geologic column, may not be as ancient as conventional radiometric dating techniques once indicated.

Coal samples, *"millions-of-years"* old by conventional dating methods, should be ^{14}C dead, but they are not. In 1988, physicist Robert H. Brown reported on the unexpected presence of ^{14}C in coal seams conventionally dated in multi-million-year time zones.

"Infinite age' samples such as anthracite coal from deep mines in Carboniferous geologic formations (270-350 million years conventional age assignment) have yielded

AMS C-14 ages in the 40,000-year range at laboratories in Europe, Canada, and the U.S.A." [6]

Similarly, *"Paleozoic and Mesozoic coal and oil dates with the Accelerator Mass Spectrometer (AMS) method …give maximum ages between 50,000 and 70,000 years. This indicates that they still have ^{14}C and seem to be younger than 70,000 years."* [7]

© Matt Trommer

England's Stonehenge testifies to human skills in ancient time.

Using the AMS method and calculating ^{14}C's half-life at 5730 years, John R. Baumgardner's 2003 findings recognized the raw measurement of the $^{14}C/^{12}C$ ratio improved from about *"…1% of the modern value to about 0.001%, extending the theoretical range of sensitivity from about 40,000 years to about 90,000 years."* [8]

Baumgardner obtained ten test coal samples from the U.S. Department of Energy Coal Sample Bank: *"…three coals from the Eocene part of the geological record, three from the Cretaceous, and four from the Pennsylvanian."* [8]

The ten samples represented a 200-million-year time spread in conventional geological time. The coal should be ^{14}C dead given the AMS limits of the 90,000-year measurement for traces of ^{14}C.

Instead of confirming absence of detectable levels of ^{14}C, the AMS tests disclosed *"…remarkably similar values of 0.26 percent modern carbon (pmc) for*

Eocene, 0.21 pmc for Cretaceous, and 0.23 pmc for Pennsylvanian … little difference in ^{14}C level as a function of position in the geological record." [8]

Within currently conventional assumptions, discrepancies astound!

"…Penguins living in the Antarctic today have yielded 3000 year old carbon 14 ages …Seals killed recently have ages of 1000 years…" [5]

"Living mollusk shells have been dated by the C-14 method at up to 2,300 years…a freshly killed seal at 1,300 years, and wood from a growing tree at 10,000 years." [9]

Radiometric dating discontinuity does nothing to ratify evolution's deep-time crutch!

Radiometric dating errors of a fossil can be compounded when the assumed date of death of the fossil is based on the radiometric date of the burial site matter and the erroneous assumption is transposed and used to date a similar fossil at another global site.

Assumption based extrapolation represents circular reasoning.

Uranium-Thorium-Lead, Rubidium-Strontium, and Potassium-Argon dating methods can generate discordant dates from identical test samples.

Gunter Faure warned of such *discordance* in isotope geology.

"Unquestionably, 'discordance' of mineral dates is more common than concordance…the mineral dates generally are not reliable indicators of the age of the rock.

"Although examples of nearly concordant U, Th-Pb dates can be found in the literature…in most cases U-and Th-bearing significance is questionable." [10]

Richard Leakey discovered what he believed to be a human skull in Kenya below rock assumed to be securely dated at 2.6 million years BP. Radiometric dating of the KBS Tuff site ranged in erratic extremes from 0.52 million BP to 17.5 million BP. [11]

Was Leakey's burial site find correctly dated at 2.6 million years BP?

Was the fossil assigned an age based upon the assumed age of the burial site, or was the site assigned a date tied to the conjectured age of the fossil?

Is either assigned date accurate?

© David H. Seymour

"Since formations we study today inherit radioisotope features from previous formations (erosion processes forming sediments; volcanic process forming igneous deposits), there is uncertainty as to how much of the daughter-product concentration in the formations we study accumulated during the geologic lifetime of those formations, and how much of the current daughter-product concentration was inherited from their source material.

"The well-defined starting point for radioisotope age determination does not assure a relationship between the radioisotope 'age' and the geological age (true time of existence) of a specimen." [12]

Discordant dating plagues Hawaiian Island time measurements. Using the potassium-argon method, ages ranging from 160 million to 2.96 billion years for lava flows that occurred in the year 1800[1] have been obtained. [13]

A cross-section of lava specimens taken from New Zealand's Mt. Ngauruhoe volcanic eruptions in 1949, 1954, and 1975 show potassium-argon dates ranging from a more recent 270,000 years BP to a distant 3,500,000 years in the past. [14]

When twenty-seven Brahma amphibolite samples of Grand Canyon basalt lava were collected from comparable sites and submitted to two *"well-credentialed internationally-recognized, commercial laboratories for radioisotope analysis,"* the results indicated pronounced discordance.

"When the calculated error margins are taken into account the different radioisotope dating methods yield completely different 'ages' that cannot be reconciled---1240±84Ma (Rb-Sr), 1655±40 Ma (Sm-Nd), and 1833±53 Ma (Pb-Pb).

"The K-Ar model 'ages' are so widely divergent from one another (ranging from 405.1±10 Ma to 2574.2±73 Ma), even from very closely spaced samples from the same outcrop of the same original lava flow, as to be useless for 'dating' any event…

"Irreconcilable disagreement within and between the methods is the norm, even at the outcrop scale. This is a devastating 'blow' to the long ages that are foundational to uniformitarian geology and evolutionary biology." [15]

Radiometric dating's discordance is not shocking given tectonic dislocation of continents and radical magnetic pole shifts. Discordance lurks as an open secret, out-of-sync with time-certain events.

Many deep time calibrations offer imprecise approximations that can't guarantee the absolute. Nor does [14]Carbon dating explain soft-tissue discovered in fossils imagined to be many millions of years old.

Conventional geochronology took a jolt in 2004 when respected paleontologist, Mary H. Schweitzer, reported the discovery of soft-tissue inside a fragment of a dinosaur femur unearthed in Montana.

Implications sent rippling waves across time projections, real and imagined. [16]

"Mary Schweitzer found fresh T. Rex femurs in 1991 and 2000, and a hadrosaur femur with blood cells in 2009. She told Science in 1993, 'it was exactly like looking at a slice of modern bone.

"But, of course, I couldn't believe it. The bones, after all, are 65 million years old. How could blood cells survive that long?'" [17]

What about those alleged 65 million-year-old *"highly fibrous… flexible…resilient"* T. *rex* fossil fragments displaying *"blood cells?"*

"Blood cells" avoiding decay for 65 million years?

Billed as *"unquestionably one of the most unexpected and important dinosaur discoveries of all time,"* the début of *Leonardo,* a mummified hadrosaur, raised academic eyebrows!

More than a composite of *"scattered collagen fibers,"* the long-extinct reptile displayed *"skin pattern and stomach contents…discernable,"* with *"whole tissues---in fact its whole body---still intact!"* [18]

Supposedly having lived and died 77 million years ago, *Lenny's* remains defy conventional time-frame expectations. This, with other recent discoveries, runs counter to multi-million-year scenarios for life-on-earth.

Collagen protein supposedly turns to dust within 30,000 years. But now its been reported that some collagen has been found as *"fossil"* material.

"DNA is particularly prone to decay, yet ancient fossil 'plants, bacteria, mammals, Neanderthals, and other archaic humans have had short aDNA sequences identified." [19]

Dinosaurs presumably went extinct 65 or 66 million years before the present, leaving behind only fossil remnants. Then along comes *Dakota,* a hippo-sized, duck-billed hadrosaur, unearthed by teenager Tyler Lawson on his family's North Dakota property in 1999. [20]

Apparently *Dakota* didn't get the word that multi-millions of years of fossilization is more than enough time to erase all traces of organic matter.

Instead, Phil Manning's University of Manchester *"team found that although the proteins that made up the hadrosaur's skin had degraded, the amino acid building blocks that once made up the proteins were still present. They believe that the dinosaur fell into a watery grave, with little oxygen present to speed along the decay process."* [21]

In the words of the astonished Dr. Manning, *"You're looking at cell-like structures; you slice through this and you're looking at the cell structure of dinosaur skin. That is absolutely gobsmacking."* [21]

There's more to the story! The *"gobsmacking"* picture conflicts with a sacred cow critical to conventional science interpretations!

Could organic material survive 66 million years after the date of death and burial---that's 660,000 centuries of 100 years per?

Then along comes Shixue Hu of China's Chengdu Geological Center reporting discovery of a fossil cemetery of 20,000 fossils, many fully intact, buried fifty feet deep in a Luoping mountain in southwestern China.

Duly awarded a 250 million year age, the treasure trove of antiquity included stunning evidence out-of-kilter with traditional evolution. Rather than life forms radically different than today's fossil world, clams, oysters, snails, and the coelacanth testify to stasis.

But the stunner was the *"soft tissues"* found on some of the fossils!!! [22]

"Soft tissues" that escaped decay for 250 million years? Really?

Either dating methodology needs major-league fine-tuning or dinosaurs walked the planet more recently than imagined.

The question follows: does it make sense to assign fossil remains the same age as the surrounding burial site matter just to accommodate evolution's geologic column?

Circular reasoning projects bootstrap science---a conclusion based on conjecture. It may contribute to a fictitious paper trail, but it delivers nothing more than a subjective guess derived from extrapolation, founded upon subjective assumption.

The persistent challenge is to objectively ascertain geo-chronological time zones not tainted with mega-million-year bias.

"Surprising as it may seem, the only real evidence for the geological succession of life, as represented by the timetable, is found in the mind of the geologist and on the paper upon which the chart is drawn. Nowhere in the earth is the complete succession of fossils found as they are portrayed in the chart..." [23]

Does the radioisotope age characteristic of the rock that enshrouds a fossil cemetery always represent the actual date of the death and burial event?

Since the answer is an obvious "no," evolution theory is deprived of an already fragile hope for salvaging any semblance of scientific substance. Darwin's evolution dream remains nothing more nor less than what its always been---a primitive, superstitious philosophy, scientifically unproven.

Evolution's time card is a joker!

II

"Let there be light..."

Timelines

*"I know this world is ruled by infinite intelligence. Everything that surrounds us -
everything that exists - proves that there are infinite laws behind it.
There can be no denying this fact. It is mathematical in its precision."* [1]

Thomas A. Edison

**Ancient civilizations devised
stone sun dials to calibrate time.**

Creation week marked the beginning of all life on earth. The first creation week miracle banished darkness.

It is no coincidence that on the first day of creation week the presence of God's Spirit introduced light and banished darkness on that blob of water-covered matter, drifting in cosmic space. The light that surrounded earth at the beginning of creation week announced the presence and the power of *"the Spirit of God hovering over the waters,"* [3] independent of the sun.

Creation of the sun and the Solar System was deferred until day four.

This day one demonstration of authority introducing creation week, confirmed God's presence and His pre-eminence as the source of universal light, energy, matter and life.

Had the sun been created on that first day rather than deferred until day four, humans might have been more readily enticed into bowing to the inanimate servant sun rather than worshipping the Master Creator of all things.

Rather than meaningless, empty worship of a fictitious sun god and inanimate objects carved from wood and stone, near-sighted human minds drifted from truth, overlooking the origin and essence of life. Eventually, blinded by sight of the sun's raging inferno, some cultures chose to worship solar power while ignoring the celestial furnace was put in place and stoked perpetually by the Creator.

No inanimate object, stone idol or graven image deserves worship! Instead, God reserved a weekly day in time for mankind to rest from physical labor and to cherish the honor of being created in God's image.

By lighting a darkness-saturated earth by the arrival of God's Spirit, before the sun even existed, the case was made that the living God is the source of all light and life.

Christ assured humans of access to the same power source that created the sun. *"You are the light of the world…Let your light shine before men, that they may see your good deeds and praise your Father in heaven."* [4]

So it wasn't until day four of creation week that *"God said, 'Let there be lights in the expanse of the sky to separate the day from the night, and let them serve as signs to mark season and days and years."* [5] This stellar event included creation of a heaven full of visible stars with a planetary system circling the sun.

More than dividing darkness from light, sun power sustains a living ecosystem; delivers unseen rays; controls climate; drives photosynthesis; filters water; cleans air; and provides earthlings with a reliable methodology for calibrating time.

Identification of a cosmic instant requires light focusing on a moving target. In the blink of an eye, constantly shifting light changes the "now" of the present to history's past tense "then." Earth-based chronology lacks the capacity to capture and identify a cosmic instant of universal time.

From earth's perspective, measurements of time, motion, speed and distance relate to light. Days, months, seasons, years and light-year distances correlate the here and "now" with history's "then."

While humans crave knowledge, attempts to pinpoint the precise moment of earth's birthday challenges finite thought capacity! Curiosity propels minds to dig deeper in a quest to understand life's origin, purpose, and direction.

Just how far back in ancient time zones did the Blue Planet and its proliferation of life first début?

Attempts to measure unlimited stretches of uncharted past time, strains comprehension. The enigma of pre-history extends beyond thought horizons while inspiring major modicums of faith. Universal time flows perpetually as an infinite flat line unless the Creator-God, the Designer of all time clocks, provides cohesion to the equation.

Internet

Internet

Internet

"God made…the greater light to govern the day!" [6]

In sync with the push and pull of the moon, ocean waves roll to shore at an average of twenty-six per minute, come rain, shine or wind. [7]

© Jeff Krushinski

"God made...the lesser light to govern the night." [6]

In the universal scheme of things, there is no such thing as time apart from a simultaneous "now" instant. Ultimately, the core issue relating to earth's age and life's origin, is based on belief, or non-belief, in an infinite, all-knowing, all-powerful, Creator God.

The speed of dark can't be measured. Darkness is simply the absence of light and is useless in computing time.

Tucked in a galaxy of precision, humans measure the time of day, relying on earth's turning on its axis, orbiting around the sun.

Readily identifiable *days* and *years* provide a measurement tailor-made for human comprehension. There would be no such thing as days, months, or years to measure time on Planet Earth, without the sun's light, the moon, and the "night clock" based on the precision of stars and constellations spinning around the North Star in a predictable east-to-west rotation.

Earth's time measurement technology is unique to this planet, without relevance beyond its celestial niche.

Time doesn't "fly" the same way on other planets in our Solar System, much less in an infinite cosmos, without known boundaries, cluttered as it is with billions of spheres, all rotating in synchronized orbits. Since all Solar System planets spin in appreciably variant cycles, an instant on earth doesn't equate with time measurement on sister planets Venus or Mars.

Mayans devised a calendar accurate to December 21, 2012. Long before access to computer technology, ancient minds *calculated the length of a year as 365.2420 days long* astonishingly close to the modern astronomical time of 365.2422 days. [8]

The all-knowing, eternal and infinite, Lord God Almighty, could have created all matter and living things at His command, in the blink of an eye. Instead, to help humans recognize His power and love, He designed the sequential process in a time environment, easy to understand.

The Genesis narrative depicts *original, unborrowed* and *underived* life created within the context of an irreducibly complex ecosystem built upon earth's *"formless and empty"* matter when *"darkness"* covered *"the surface of the deep."* [9]

At the command of the Creator, a fully functioning ecosystem complete with light, oxygen based atmosphere, dry land capable of supporting vegetation, the Plant Kingdom, along with the Solar System, were put in place in the universe during the first four days of that miraculous week.

The Animal Kingdom, with birds and fish, followed on day five with land animals, and humans, the crowning achievement designed in God's image and given dominion over the earth, on day six.

Day seven was reserved for the celebration of perfection.

Ever since day four, not only does sunshine chase darkness away every 24-hours when it dawns in the east and sets in the west, it paints the landscape with a kaleidoscope of dazzling colors guaranteed to brighten human psyches.

This daily show is but a hint of what that "lucky ol' sun" does to enhance plant and animal life on earth. Earth's proximity to the sun impacts climate.

Raindrops result from sun induced evaporation. The world's food supply is contingent upon the sun doing its thing.

The regular night/day sequence plays to human need for regular rest. Sleep comes naturally when darkness swallows the sun's rays.

Time calibration is based on earth-days and relative distances tied to the speed of light. Measurement of time by days, and the cycle for earth to orbit the sun provides a readily recognized time calculation.

A ray of earth-bound sunshine, traveling at 186,282 miles per second, takes 8 light minutes to reach our planet. By conventional comparisons, some galaxies are estimated to be more than 13 billion light years distant. While intergalactic distance calibrations are subject to interpretation and error, the mind staggers at the implication.

This giant fireball delivers life-sustaining power to earth, fueled every day by what seems to be a limitless supply of atomic energy. Moving through space in a path so precise that its location can be pin-pointed hundreds of years in the past and predicted a thousand years into the future, its reliability is not subject to question.

Planet Earth seems designed to be an on-going adventure for human beings to be challenged by the infinite complexity of nature and the unfathomable *"mystery of Godliness."* [10]

The Lord God Almighty is just, all loving,

all-powerful, omniscient, omnipresent, and eternal.

He pre-existed His creation of all things!

Its axiomatic that the universe brimming with billions of stars, galaxies and constellations, millions of light years distant from Planet Earth, pre-existed creation of life on earth. Nothing in Scripture suggests the contrary.

The Bible does suggest angels pre-existed creation of life on earth

Job 38:7 describes the moment *"when the morning stars sang together and all the angels shouted for joy"* celebrating the creation event. Augustine cites a *"super-celestial society,"* as existing prior to the creation of humans.

The Scripture makes no claim the entire universe was created during the week God created life on earth.

With the sun created to sustain life and to compute time, combined with the moon's tide-pulling magic, the Solar System took its place in space on day four of creation week.

The phrase *"he made the stars also"* can be understood to mean a reference to God's eternal power and a recognition that the stars in the universe existed already. Given the relation of the North Star to earth, the phrase could also mean that stars visible to earth were created on day four.

Earth's axis points northward within one degree of Polaris. The North Star would be a logical component of the fourth day creation event, along with the multitude of visible stars within its sphere of influence. Polaris, with the array of stars seeming to spin around it, provides travelers with dependable directions while complementing the sun's cosmic time machine.

Like a beacon shining from what appears to be a relatively fixed position in the northern sky, this brightest star in the Ursa Minor constellation provides navigators a dependable GPS (Global Positioning System). Searches for other stars in the cosmos typically begin with the North Star.

Prior to the United States Civil War, runaway slaves looked heavenward for directions, encouraged to "follow the drinking gourd" to freedom.

With this mathematically complex system in motion at the close of day four, the stage was set for the creation of all animal life and human species.

No human being walking today's earth witnessed earth's birth. While the brightest minds can't pinpoint the exact date of life's earthly birthday, the weekly day of rest, commemorates the event by honoring the Creator.

Perception of time involves something vastly more significant than an abstract issue providing intellectual fodder for debate. The Big Picture significance of life is the on stage feature in the theater of the universe.

Why would the infinite, all-powerful Creator set in motion an easy-read time calibration tied to earth's orbit on its axis around the sun, and then inspire an account of origins that discarded real *days*, leaving human imaginations to decipher the abstract?

God created humans on a pedestal of privilege, positioned to enjoy a relationship built on regular and direct communication with the Creator. More than a superficial article of philosophical faith, to accept or reject intellectually, real religion opens the heart and soul to a relationship that permeates and enriches every fiber of the being.

The Genesis account sets aside a one-day-in-seven interlude for humans to fest from physical labor and to remember the privilege of being created in God's image. The fourth commandment set aside the weekly day of rest from labor by reminding, *"you were slaves in Egypt"* and that *"the Lord your God brought you out of there."* [11]

The weekly rest cycle guarantees a barrier to involuntary subservience with the reminder that all humans are created equal. Once evil intruded by corrupting creation and subverting the weekly memorial honoring the Creator, exploitation of the labor of other humans emerged as a fact of life, evolving a slavery system that infected and destroyed entire cultures!

© Joyce Boffert

**Monarch butterflies brightened the landscape
on day five of creation week.**

Despite allegiance pledged to the declaration *" all men are created equal,"* early in the formative years of the United States, Darwin's sinister demeaning of some human cultures provided political cover for exploitation of the barbaric slave trade.

The industry's callous tentacles spanned the Atlantic, unloading manacled human cargoes in New World sanctuaries. The brutal virus carried a bitter price, above and beyond the ruthless disposal of human lives on public auction blocks.

The savage excesses of the slavery curse lingered to eventually rip the heart from the fledgling American republic. As a consequence of the slave traffic, 620,000 Americans of all races and colors lost their lives in the searing anguish of a Civil War blood bath.

Two years after Darwin published *Origin of Species*, Thaddeus Stevens, Vice-president of the Confederacy, touted slavery as *"the proper status of the negro in our form of civilization…the negro is not equal to the white man; that slavery, subordination to the superior race, is his natural and moral condition."* [12]

Less than ten years after Darwin went public in 1859 with his survival of the fittest racism, this persistent band of recalcitrants left no doubt as to their commitment and bluntly-stated intent. Still smarting from the suppression of the rebellion, an influential cadre of white political figures expressed resentment in pointed terms that might have made Darwin blush.

"A superior race is put under the rule of an inferior race…The white people of our State will never quietly submit to negro rule. This is a duty we owe to the proud Caucasian race, whose sovereignty on earth God has ordained." [13]

Words of hate presaged a campaign of terror and murder. Darwin didn't start the Civil War. But the fall-out from his theory offered faux cover while contaminating core human values and disgracing history!

Creation week's day seven was set-aside as a celebratory event, commemorating rights and duties for all humans created in God's image.

Deep time caught the attention of theistic evolutionists offering lip service to a Creator while simultaneously dismissing the Genesis account of creation week as mere metaphor, laced with symbolic spiritual messages.

Theistic purveyors of compromise dismiss literal days of creation week as *"symbolic;"* insisting the story of a flood *"covering the entire globe"* was less that worldwide. Their Christian allegiance is polluted with junk "science" rather than absolute faith in the Scripture's *"thus saith the Lord."*

Dismissing the Genesis account of creation week's literal days as *symbolic, allegory,* or *metaphor,* mocks the majestic beauty of the event. Arbitrarily scrambling natural time landmarks as symbolism, merely to accommodate evolution theory, diminishes the Creator's role and defaces the Big Picture of life's purpose and meaning.

Proposing creation week days symbolize open stretches of indeterminate time, undercuts the core essence of the weekly rest day.

Theistic religionists attempt to bridge an unbridgeable gap.

Swallowing junk "science" bait, theistic evolution trashes the Biblical narrative of creation by injecting a disconnect between the tragedy of evil's origin and Christ's plan of redemption with its promise of life eternal.

One typical assertion of a theistic evolutionist asserts, *"there is no doubt that life (and death) has been on this planet for millions of years;"* while avowing evidence exists *"for the presence of humans over at least 100,000 years."* [14]

Attempts to mix evolution conjecture with Christian faith substitutes academic scam for Scriptural authority. Its less than logical to suggest the Creator put the sun's observable time measurement in place only to play a game of "gotcha," confusing humans with a Genesis account identifying the creation week *days* as abstract *metaphors* or *symbols.*

In a vain quest to find a cosmetic commonality with the Bible, theistic evolutionists embrace schlock science and discard Biblical supremacy for a cosmetically compromised Christian faith, adorned with slick-sounding phrases!

Disciples of theological Pied Pipers have been horn swoggled! It's an either/or choice, not an *"I feel strongly both ways"* option.

The Sabbath-day rest described in Exodus 20:8-11 identifies a literal, weekly, 24-hour day of rest to honor the Creator and to celebrate the miracle of life. Deuteronomy 5: 12-15 restated the command to rest as a weekly reminder of Divine deliverance from dawn-to-dusk, slave labor.

The Deuteronomy reference replicated the Exodus command to rest one literal day each week, correlating with the fourth commandment of Exodus and the Genesis account of a literal, seven-day creation week.

Demoting the Divinely ordered weekly rest day to "symbolic" status, corrupts its significance and subverts God's authority. Why would Genesis creation *days* be metaphor while Deuteronomy and Exodus memorialize creation with weekly, literal-time rest *days?*

Christ confirmed, *"The Sabbath was made for man."* [15]

If only metaphor, God's guarantee of a literal day of physical rest each week would offer little comfort to exhausted former slaves who survived the searing heat of Egyptian *"iron-melting furnaces."* [16]

It makes no sense to suggest the 24-hour day earmarked for physical rest and celebration is a metaphor for an abstract stretch of time longer than a human life! Promising "symbolic" rest from physical labor spouts hollow rhetoric, and a distortion of obvious, Biblical meaning.

Theistic evolution mischaracterizes the all-powerful Lord God Almighty, Creator of the universe and Author of all true science as a fabricator of benign myths and pious platitudes.

Finite minds struggle to comprehend and calibrate infinite time and space. Concepts of time without beginning or end, and cosmic space without boundaries, staggers mortal intellects.

So the nagging question persists: "Within the human perception of time in the context of days, weeks, and years---does radiometric dating provide reliable evidence that life on earth originated millions of years BP?"

III

Day One

Young Life, Old Earth

*"Ultimately, the Darwinian theory of evolution
is no more nor less than the great cosmogenic myth
of the twentieth century."* [1]

Michael Denton

© Alex Edmonds

**One of California's Giant Sequoias shows tree rings
reaching 3500 years before the present.**

When Washington State's Mt. St. Helens blew its top, torrents of hyper-heated ash engulfed and destroyed wholesale quantities of plant and animal life---including *Homo sapiens.*

Where a proud mountain peak once dominated, a concave chasm confirmed the reality of nature's catastrophic reach, exploding on a date certain---8:32 a.m., May 18, 1980.

Human casualties from the explosion included Harry Truman (an old time mountain man, not to be confused with a former U.S. President), who ignored warnings of impending danger. His vaporized remains have never been seen since.

While the real-time record of the 1980 event stands undisputed, initial radiometric data of the lava dome conflicts, out-of-kilter.

"Rocks formed in and subsequent to the 1980 eruption …should date 'too young to measure'…According to radioisotope dating, certain minerals in the lava dome are up to 2.4 million years old.

"All of the minerals combined yield the date of 350,000 years by the potassium-argon technique," despite the fact, *"these minerals and the rocks that contain them cooled within lava between the years 1980 and 1986."* [2]

A 350,000 to 2.4 million-year time stretch shouts discordance!

The discrepancy highlights a fossil-dating dilemma.

It's certifiable fact mountain man Harry Truman, lost his life in May, 1980.

Mt. St. Helens following its 1980 eruption.

Just because the radiometric age allocated the turf surrounding his remains is dated 350,000 or 2.4 million years before the present, doesn't mean Truman lived and died 350,000 or 2.4 million years ago!

The conclusion seems obvious: Harry Truman lost his life in May, 1980, regardless of the projected radiometric dates assigned to the fall-out residue from the volcanic event of that date!

This reality wreaks havoc with evolution's dubious technique of awarding fossils the radiometric date of the matter composing the burial site. No one suggests Mount St. Helen's Harry Truman lived and died 350,000 years before the present.

Fossils of plant and animal life forms that lived and died several thousand years before the present could be buried in matter showing radiometric dates millions of deep time years BP.

Relying on radiometric dating of inorganic matter to determine the age of the fossil remains of an organic life form, willfully ignores the fact fossils don't assume the date age of the surrounding burial site turf.

**Its less than logical to equate a plant or animal's
date of death with the radiometric age of the
burial site matter surrounding the fossil.**

No question about it, both earth's *inorganic matter* and its plethora of organic *life forms* had a *Time Zero* beginning. Genesis describes a lifeless, inert blob of matter, covered with water, floating in dark space at the beginning of creation week.

"Now the earth was formless and empty, darkness was over the surface of the deep, and the Spirit of God was hovering over the waters." [3]

No reference is made to the creation of water or inorganic raw material during the week God created life. Nor does the Bible date the exact moment life was created or the length of time a blob of inert, water-covered matter floated in darkness prior to the creation event.

Ideas split as to the *how, where* and *when*. One observer, not a Bible scholar apologist, reports *"evidence showing that, 3.5 billion years ago, Earth was mostly covered by water."* [4]

Taking the Genesis narrative to mean what it says, God created all plant and animal life, with a supporting ecosystem, during the first six days of a literal week of seven days.

"Formless and empty" matter provided the foundation upon which God created life---*original, unborrowed* and *underived.* An already existing universe celebrated the event *"When the morning stars sang together, and all the sons of God shouted for joy."* [5]

The implication is clear: several thousand years before the present, there was a *Time Zero* moment God's command introduced life, together with a global ecosystem that miraculously transformed the face of formless matter into the Blue Planet, throbbing with young plant and animal life!

Physicist Robert H. Brown interprets the Bible account to mean what it says: a lifeless mass, inundated with water, cloaked in a blanket of darkness. He describes the possibility of *"radioactive decay over hundreds of millions of years prior to Creation Week"* as feasible, taking Genesis 1:2 to mean what it says.

"New Testament writers make it absolutely clear that all components of the physical universe were created by God, but do not specify a time frame. The only necessary basic time specifications are provided in the first 11 chapters of Genesis. And those specifications apply only to living organisms and the environment that supports them.

"Nothing is said in the Bible about time in connection with the creation of water or the creation of the inorganic material that was raised above surface water on the third day of Creation Week---these components are simply stated as being 'there' at the beginning of Creation Week." [6]

The Bible doesn't express or imply gradualism!

Twentieth century biologist, Frank Lewis Marsh, suggested all earth's life forms were likely created in a fully mature format, imbued with an appearance of age, thriving as components of a complete, fully functioning, irreducibly complex ecosystem.

"Our earth was created, along with the living forms with which it was furnished, with an appearance of age." [7]

**California's Giant Sequoias grow as high as 311 feet---longer
than the length of a football field---with diameters as wide as 56 feet.
Compare the size of the man standing between the trees.**

Adam did not arrive as a helpless infant, but walked the planet as a fully-grown human, caring for himself and capable of reproduction. He required food to sustain life---not just seeds to sow. Food crops grew in place, ripe and ready to eat.

Without plants and trees bursting with fruits and vegetables, Adam would have starved.

Mature trees stretched toward the sky; fish swam; birds flew; flowers bloomed; vegetation flourished; and animals roamed.

The volcanic island of Surtsey, just south of Iceland, first surfaced the Atlantic Ocean, November 14, 1963. A casual observer might mistake the landmark to be several thousand years old.

Less than four years after its appearance, a paleontologist flew to the site to inspect the pristine landscape, later reporting its appearance of age. [8]

He saw a brand-new chunk of raw geography projecting a weatherworn appearance. A relentless sea had ground out black sand beaches. Multi-layered cliffs, composed of a series of lava flows, guarded a four-mile coastline, carved randomly by Atlantic tides. Foot-long stalactites hang from cave ceilings. Basalt blocks appear as rounded boulders, chiseled by the elements.

 Despite its tender 1963 age, sea gulls, insects, and at least three species of plants already called Surtsey home.

© Chuck Nelson

God is not limited to a single creative event in the context of infinite time. Christ, the Creator, [9] possesses the power to create earth's life forms in an instant or in real-time days. Anything less and He would not be the all-knowing, all-powerful, all-loving God, worthy of human worship.

When humans attempt to recreate God in their own image, they distort, disparage and diminish the majestic power and authority of the one eternal, infinite, just, all-loving Lord God Almighty who created all things.

Aurelius Augustinus (Augustine, 354-430 A.D.), Bishop of Hippo and Christian intellectual, played an influential role in the African Synod of Hippo (393 A.D), which confirmed the Biblical Canon.

Prolific writer and dynamic Christian leader, Augustine quoted liberally from both Old and New Testaments. Committed to the integrity of the creation miracle, Augustine attributed the Genesis narrative to the pen of Moses, writing under God's inspiration.

The words of Moses, a commanding presence with giant intellect and charismatic leadership skills, warrant serious attention and sober respect. In today's academic era insisting on the authority of primary source material, the unmatched credentials of Moses stand tall!

He grew up in the privileged environment of the Egyptian royal family ruling an empire that straddled ancient world trade routes. On at least two occasions, at the burning bush and on Mt. Sinai, Moses communicated directly with God, learning the Genesis narrative from the Creator.

 Level granite surfaces in Egyptian pyramids were trimmed to a tolerance of $2/1000^{th}$ of an inch; deep rectangles were carved with square corners; and circular holes were drilled through the face of solid rock leaving geometrically precise, cylindrical openings.

The identity of the tools and the millenniums-old technology baffles scholars! *"It may be…that the science we see at the dawn of recorded history was not science at its dawn…*[but] *remnants of the science of some great… civilization."* [10]

Egypt's Giza Pyramids

Exposed to impressive Egyptian culture that survives antiquity, higher education would have been unsurpassed with its records of ancient and contemporary civilizations carved in stone and painted on rolls of papyrus.

More than indoctrinated with state-of-the-art wisdom of the ages, Moses learned the culture of the Hebrews at the feet of his mother, Jochebed.

The pivotal life and times of Noah would have deserved front-and-center billing. This historic figure of living faith, walked and talked with humans sharing eyewitness accounts of events that extended years before, during, and after the global deluge.

Methuselah's life span, a descendant seven generations down from Adam, would have overlapped with both Adam and Noah. Not only did Noah live both before and after the global deluge, but his life, and the life of his son would have overlapped with that of Abraham.

Moses was the beneficiary of a cultural narrative built on both written records and eyewitness accounts. In contrast to the vagaries of tradition, Moses' words reflect the "best evidence rule."

Already a powerhouse source of ancient history, Moses' credentials and writings were authenticated under the inspiration of the Creator Himself. From the "burning bush" communication to Mount Sinai's summit, Moses wrote with authority, including the Genesis summary of creation week.

Writing in 1654 A.D., Bishop James Ussher, distinguished scholar and clergyman, proposed creation week to have occurred in 4004 B.C. based on Genesis genealogy.

Since the time lapse from creation week to man's fall and eviction from the Garden of Eden is not defined in Genesis, a speculative question arises: Was Adam's age calculated from the moment of his creation or after being barred from access to the tree-of-life with onset of his physical aging?

Humans don't know the answer nor is it necessary to know!

Whether or not the Ussher chronology offers the last word in dating the creation of life on earth, above and beyond his academic skills and the authenticity of his primary source material, there is evidence in both nature and archaeology suggesting life on earth originated only thousands, not millions of years in the past.

Some creationist scholars believe several "thousand" years might be added to Ussher's estimated 6,000 years BP but not "millions."

For a variety of reasons, Ussher's genealogical scenario is entitled to thoughtful evaluation, not to be dismissed out-of-hand.

For one thing, the scholarship and integrity of Moses deserves respect.

For another, the extended lifetimes of humans from Adam through the pre-global flood era lends plausibility to eyewitness accounts descriptive of events both before and after the worldwide deluge.

Recognizing the brilliance and longevity of ancient humans, it is most likely written records were put in place to preserve history of noteworthy events both before and after the flood.

Apart from the slightly different time variations offered by the Septuagint version of Genesis, one possible deficiency of Ussher's chronology, is that the Hebrew word *"ab,"* translated *"father,"* can also mean *"grandfather"* or *"ancestor."* But that can be argued either way.

For example, Genesis 10 describes Shem as *"…the father of all the children of Eber," while* Genesis 11 confirms a two generation gap between Shem and Eber, indicating the word translated *"father"* can mean *"ancestor."*

While Ussher never claimed infallibility, his carefully crafted analysis of the Genesis genealogical record combines a perspective of antiquity with an insightful look at the big picture meaning of human life. Skeptics challenging Ussher's thesis note Biblical chronology doesn't exist before Abraham and genealogy is an inadequate substitute for chronology.

Still, critics have nothing remotely comparable to offer.

Archaeology and natural science provide glimpses of antiquity. Measured in thousands-of-years, and not millions, recorded history offers no evidence confirming evolution-in-action.

Whether or not the Ussher chronology offers the last word in the dating of creation of life on earth, there is evidence in both nature and archaeology that deserves consideration in support of his analysis.

Evidence of plant life reaching back 4,000 years before the present tracks with Ussher's dating the global flood some 4300+ years ago.

Plant and animal life, virtual mirror images of today's fauna and flora, flourished without a hint of evolution in action.

Egyptian mummies represent four *Homo sapiens* blood types, identical to what flows through the veins of twenty-first century humans.

"Methuselah," a scrawny bristlecone pine clinging to the rugged slopes of the Sierra Mountains, survives today, rooted in more than 4,000 years of earth's immediate past. A Giant Sequoia carries rings confirming its life began 3500 years before the present.

"The fact that even the Great Pyramid at Giza, which according to modern historians is only supposed to date from approximately 2,600 BC, can contain such a remarkable wealth of a mathematical, astronomical, and the geophysical information (it not only contains the value of pi, and is aligned with Sirius, but it's dimensions accurately describe the major measurements of the Earth) indicates that there was an immense scholastic tradition in Egypt by 2600 BC...

"Even if we were to assume that ancient Egypt like the Druidic priesthood relied to a large extent on oral tradition, the fact of architectural construction, mathematical ingenuity, and astronomical prediction and calculation, indicates a library tradition to both compute, research, and convey lore, knowledge and wisdom from generation to generation." [11]

These projected dates correlate comfortably with the date of the global flood as calculated by the Bishop's Biblical-based chronology.

The Bible reports that following the flood, descendants of Noah, speaking the same language, congregated on the Plain of Shinar, intending to build a tower tall enough to spare them from the death and devastation of future floods. To halt construction and to disperse the population, God confused *"their language"* so they could not *"understand each other."* [12]

Subsequently, diverse written languages were developed.

The Hebrew alphabet originated at least 3500 years BP. [13]

Between the years 2100-1500 BC, at least five scripts were known to be in use including Egyptian hieroglyphs, Acadian Cuneiform, hieroglyphiform syllabary of Phoenicia, the linear alphabet of Sinai, and the cuneiform alphabet of Ugarit. [13]

Standout civilizations with visible archaeological roots reach back to the Sumerian, 3500 BCE; the emergence of Egyptian power by 3000 BCE; and Indus Valley stirrings as early as 2600 BCE.

The Chinese calendar boasts antiquity. The reign of Yu, the first emperor of the first Chinese dynasty (Xia), arose BC 2205.[14] The Shang Dynasty's written history surfaces 1766 BCE.

© Izmael

Monuments of stone mark legacies of ancient civilizations.

These landmark time frames represent composite touchstones for the early beginnings of *modern history*---all since 4349 BC.

Throughout what is called modern history, evolution is a no show!

If eight humans survived a worldwide deluge only thousands of years before the present, understandably skills in working with iron, bronze and copper would have to be reintroduced. Rather than bumbling cave-man types surviving on brawn, sophisticated minds left their mark on still-visible landscapes.

Although [14]Carbon dating doesn't assure slam dunk precision, some believe, civilization's beginnings appeared at least 5500 years BP.[15]

Aware of the ice age's receding edges in Europe, archaeological tracking of recent history, has revealed traces of human habitation in Jericho, adjacent to the Mediterranean Sea, 10,000 years BP. There, in today's Turkey, remnants of sophisticated architecture still stand. [16]

From evidence he scrutinized, Charles H. Hapgood, author of *Maps of the Ancient Sea Kings*, concluded that far from the imagined successive stages of development from a primitive era of Stone, to Bronze, to Iron, ancient cultures mastered mathematics, astronomy and science.

Granite monuments from known, past civilizations confirm that ancient humans were anything but knuckle-dragging oafs who communicated with grunts. Astounded by the evidence of advanced technology in ancient times, some of those buying into the questionable IQ level of original humans wonder if "aliens" provided the know-how.

After completing analysis of a portfolio of ancient maps of the world indicating use of spherical trigonometry, Hapgood, concluded, *"in remote times, before the rise of any of the known cultures,"* there well could have been *"a true civilization, of a comparatively advanced sort…even more advanced that the civilization of Egypt, Babylonia, Greece and Rome…*

"The mapping of a continent like Antarctica implies much organization" and *"many exploring expeditions…It is unlikely that navigation and mapmaking were the only sciences by this people."* [10]

A mystery lingers as to the source of relatively accurate, ancient maps that appear to document portions of Antarctica's coast and its continental landmass before it was covered by its present ice cap.

"These older maps were based upon a sophisticated understanding of the spherical trigonometry of map projections, and---what seems even more incredible---upon a detailed and accurate knowledge of the latitudes and longitudes of coastal features throughout a large part of the world." [10]

Fossil evidence confirms that sometime in the long ago, today's ice-loaded Antarctica provided a home for a variety of plants and animals, typical of a more temperate climate.

"Abundant finds of fossil leaves and wood point to the existence of extensive forestation in earlier geological periods, even to within a few degrees of latitude of the South Pole itself.

"Dinosaurs, and later, marsupial mammals once roamed across its surface." [17]

Does this paleontological reality correlate with a relatively recent time when the *Maps of the Ancient Sea Kings* might have been charted?

Is it possible that maps charting the coast of an earlier Antarctica were charted before the deluge and preserved by Noah for post-flood times?

Could that have been a source of maritime skills that guided venturesome sailors hundreds of years into the post-flood future?

While definitive answers should be viewed as conjecture, it seems rational to assume that generations prior to and after the global flood understood sophisticated ship design and the mathematics of navigation.

Grunting gorillas, tree-hugging great apes or tree swinging monkeys lacked any minimal capacity to have mastered the techniques!

IV

Life's Slippery Slope

Devolution

"We know that the whole creation has been groaning,

as in the pains of childbirth, right up to the present time." [1]

Paul the Apostle

© Caitlin Mira

**The Second Law of Thermodynamics demonstrates its effect on
this tipsy remnant of a century-old, California ghost town.**

Designated the "Antikythera mechanism," the sophistication of the 2,000+ year-old machine with its 30 bronze gears and more than 80 fragments continues to intrigue researchers unraveling its mysteries a century after its discovery.

Even before surrendering its secrets, the delicate design suggests that far from evolution's mischaracterization of ancient humans as knuckle-dragging oafs who communicated with grunts and groans our ancestors walked, talked, and created as fully developed *Homo sapiens*.

Wikepedia

Antikythera Mechanism [2]

Contemporary scholars believe the Antikythera Mechanism, built circa 87 B.C, carries information showing the earth's relationship to the sun, our moon and the five planets recognized by the Greeks.

X-ray technology has identified inner-workings as complex as a 19th century Swiss clock that also track the Olympic year cycle.

Digging deeper into time, technological and engineering skills, carved in stone by human ancestors, continue to amaze.

These weather-beaten monuments, thousands of years old, testify that knuckle-draggers have not been on the scene for at least the last 4,000 years. Ancestor humans lived longer and were at least as intelligent as their modern counterparts.

"Egyptian civilization was not a 'development' but a 'legacy.'" [3]

Sophisticated tools used in the cutting, polishing, hauling and placing precisely shaped multi-ton blocks of granite and marble defies explanation.

Yet, there they stand, architectural masterpieces for all the world to admire. Egyptian pyramids and England's Stonehenge were not conceived and put in place by mutant amateurs.

More than massive symbolism, intricate details challenge imaginations.

What tools were used to cut square corners and long, perfectly straight rectangular grooves in the face of solid granite without trace of a chisel mark? How was it possible to polish giant slabs of marble as smooth as glass, free of flawed handiwork? And what about those precise, circular holes drilled into the hardest rock blocks?

Answers would likely have been found in one or more of those ancient libraries that no longer exist.

Asia Minor's Pergamum Library, created after the death of Alexander the Great was the geographic center for the development of parchment. This learning center reportedly contained 200,000 items. Its needless destruction deprived future access to a prized compendium of Phoenician culture, history and science.

North Africa's Carthage Library reputedly housed 500,000 items prior to its destruction by the Romans in 146 BC. And the famed Egyptian library in Alexandria, founded by Ptolemy I sometime between 323 and 283 BC, was believed to have included as many as 700,000 (some estimate a million) items until destroyed in 48 B.C. by Caesar's reckless legions.

Obliteration of these treasuries of ancient world history and scientific knowledge, eliminated ready access to accounts of ancient times and set the stage for civilization's downward spiral toward Medieval era darkness.

Rather than Darwin's predicted *"progress toward perfection,"* **history points to retrogression and devolution!**

Peer review offered no deterrent to Charles Darwin's musings. Devoid of significant academic credentials, he compiled ponderous writings based on personal opinion influenced by Grandfather Erasmus Darwin's thinking.

At the age of 50, he rushed *Origin* into print, cobbled together from personal observations during his five-year excursion aboard the HMS Beagle and his pigeon experiments conducted at his Downe family estate.

Lacking knowledge that a living cell consisted of anything more than a blob of protoplasm, much less DNA's "language of life," he released his dubious ideas fully aware the preponderance of fossil evidence didn't support his molecule-to-man imaginings. Except for a pitifully few, debatable finds, those conjectured "missing links" continue hiding

The shibboleth of some *"warm little pond"* serving as a nursery for spontaneously generating first life smacks of flat earth mentality. The guru of life by accident, admitted to *"flaws"* and *"holes"* that plagued his ideas, confiding to Asa Gray he may *"…have devoted my life to a phantasy [sic]."* [4]

Debunked and devalued, *The Origin of Species* still survives as a calcified tribute to the powers of social status, economic privilege and blind tradition in the preservation and propagation of thin-soup thinking.

"Evolutionism, or the 'theory of evolution'…is the erroneous idea that evolution is the source of progress and the cause of the cosmos structure---life and any other systems in the universe." [5]

The fossil record abounds with evidence of once thriving, giant species.

What has emerged from a century of discovery is a cross-section of gigantic fossil ancestors that dwarf replica descendants. No genealogical trail precedes the sudden appearance of these giant ancestors. Genetically complete prototypes appear fully formed and in place from time zero.

One thing is certain: a long time ago, giant species roamed earth!

Armor-plated armadillo missed Darwin's message that descendants must not only modify but also improve. Instead, today's armadillos appear to be puny versions of their nine-foot-long ancestors.

The roster of jumbo-sized ancestors features a crocodile with a seven-foot head and a fossilized, cow-sized pig housed in a Denver museum.

Tons of dinosaur bones, uncovered late in the nineteenth-century in the rugged high prairies of Colorado and Wyoming, testify to giant-sized life forms that no longer exist. Massive dinosaurs, some believed to have extended as long as 150 feet tip-to-tail, once roamed the earth.

Foothills high in the Himalayas *"contain fossil beds rich with extinct terrestrial animals, a tortoise twenty feet long, a species of elephant with tusks fourteen feet long, and three feet in circumference."* [6]

Twenty-foot-long great white sharks patrolling Pacific shores strike terror, but the fossil remains of an ancestor shark found on dry land near Oildale, California, weighed eight times as much, measured forty feet in length, and sported a twelve-foot head.

And speaking of fearsome, how about *"…The monstrous Carcharodon… possessing distinctive triangular teeth up to 8" long, [that] may have had a 6-7ft wide jaw gape, and a length of 80 ft."* [7]

Washington, D.C.'s Smithsonian displays a sloth as large as a pickup truck. Rhinoceros-sized marsupials and giant kangaroos once inhaled Australian air. Foot-long trilobites occupied what is now Morocco. Oversized lemurs hung out in Madagascar.

The Caribbean's Anguilla Island, at one time provided home base to a three hundred pound rat. Colorful dragonflies with inch-thick bodies propelled by two-and-one-half foot gossamer wings hovered over pools of cool water in some ancient past.

© Gerrit de Vries

**As fierce as this guy looks, fossil evidence suggests
the heads of his crocodile ancestors measured seven feet
on bodies forty feet long---twice the length of today's species.**

© Audrey Snider

**The fossil record reveals giant scorpions two feet in length with some
estimated to have been longer based on fossil tracks.[8]**

Australia provided homes for other now-extinct giants. Imagine a
tortoise the size of a Volkswagen Beetle; a Kangaroo ten-feet tall; or a
"wombat-like creature the size of a hippo.[9] The enormous, Australian bird,
Genyornis newtoni, makes the twenty-first century emu appear scrawny.

Elephant-sized ground sloths roamed South America.

The eye-catching list of giant-sized fossils includes a fourteen-inch tarantula…a millipede-like creature six feet long and a foot wide…a forty-foot crocodile twice the length of its living descendants…giant beavers…*eurypterids* (enormous crabs), ranked among the largest invertebrates ever…ammonites several feet in diameter…pterosaurs with wingspans reaching fifty feet…canary-size mayflies.

Fossil piranhas have been found four times the size of their ravenous descendants. Imagine the pesky cockroach, equipped with an intimidating foot-long body to better perform mischief.

Think about fossil clams spanning 12 feet across, weighing in at 650 pounds when living, discovered in the Andes 13,000 feet above sea level in the Huancavelica province of Peru.[10]

A jellyfish 28 inches in diameter that *"…must have been buried extremely rapidly…"* was discovered in a Wisconsin *"fossilized beach."* [11]

Mosses 2-3 feet high (compared to today's 1 to 3 inches) brightened the landscape; horsetail reeds grew up to 50 feet tall (ten times today's 5 to 6 feet); and a hornless rhinoceros towered 18 feet high while stretching 30 feet in length.[12]

© Kenneth Sponsier

Next time you explore California's coast, you might gaze up the trunk of the Grizzly Giant, one of a grove of still surviving descendant Sequoia trees, still stabbing up to three-hundred feet into the wild blue yonder.

Don't overlook the over five-foot long coiled shellfish (compared to 8 inches today); the eight foot wide bison skull on display at the Mt. Blanco Fossil Museum, Crosbyton, Texas; the ten-foot tall ammonite shell on display in a German museum; and turtles nearly four meters long.[13]

Finally, check out the eight-foot shell of the giant nautiloid (resembles a modern squid), [14] and the fossil footprints in Canadian sandstone believed to be those of a twenty-inch long centipede, five times the length of its mini-sized descendants.[15]

The oldest surviving written record describes oversized *Homo sapiens*. *"The Nephilim were on the earth in those days…They were heroes of old, men of renown."* [16]

After the global flood, ten of the twelve Israel spies sent to evaluate defenses in the land of Canaan, returned with a discouraging report, again citing the Nephilim.

"They are stronger than we are…All the people we saw there were of great size… We saw the Nephilim there…We seemed like grasshoppers in our own eyes, and we looked the same to them." [17]

From a simple cell creating itself accidentally in Darwin's conjectured *"warm little pond,"* evolution mischaracterizes human ancestors as stooped, knuckle-draggers, gradually evolving upright strides.

Ancient human ancestors were nothing of the kind.

Decay and deterioration of earth's life and matter highlight devolution. Wrinkles in the faces of aging humans provide a hint of things to come. Iron rusts; concrete crumbles.

Disneyworld's magic would be overgrown with weeds, worn out mechanisms and pealing paint without 24/7 maintenance.

Absent intelligent intervention, devolution, not evolution, rules!

Original life perceptions represent diametrically opposing views!

Darwin imagined that some simple, reproducing life form, created itself accidentally from non-living matter, in some *"warm little pond,"* millions of years ago. Then, incrementally, supposedly, it randomly transformed itself into every kind of plant and animal life that inhabits today's earth.

Nothing could be further from the truth!

Ever the optimist, Darwin relied on the thought processes of his own mind to piece together his *"progress toward perfection"* conjecture.

The concept remains a tortured paradox! Evolution theory, if true, came from a human brain that would have fashioned itself accidentally.

Reality points instead, to all life on earth having been designed and created perfect, pristine and pure, at the top of its game, by the command of a *"Superior Rationality,"* the Lord God Almighty.

The Scripture narrative attests to a bucolic beginning when giants thrived and humans, created in God's image, lived long lives in an environment of perfect biodiversity. When the first *Homo sapiens* couple fell victim to deceit and chose disobedience, perfection slipped into devolution's downhill patterns of decay.

The Second Law of Thermodynamics
brings inexorable deterioration of Planet Earth's ecosystem.

The Second Law's impact contributes to ecosystem decline, inflicting its relentless toll on plants, animals and all material things.

The label "evolution" has been high jacked when used to connote upside progress while the term "devolution" more accurately reflects reality. Upside-down rhetoric saturates a culture intent on giving God a bum rap.

Purveyors of neo-Darwinism commit to a materialistic faith that credits an accidental "act of nature" as the source of life. But when those same natural forces mar the landscape, knee-jerk semantics label the disaster an "act of God."

Something is out-of-kilter here!

© Robert Fullerton

**Bodie, California's battered remnants of an 1876 gold town,
decay at the thin-air altitude of 8,379 feet.**

Earth, with its teeming biodiversity, should be attributed to the creative act of an all-powerful God, deserving worship, while the destructive forces of hurricanes, earthquakes, floods, and tornadoes should be recognized as acts of rampaging nature.

According to the First Law of Thermodynamics, energy can neither be created nor destroyed. The Second Law of Thermodynamics is qualitative, confirming the tendency of energy to flow away, to disperse from concentration in a single, localized place.

Entropy is the quantitative measure of the dispersion or spreading out of the qualitative. It represents a measure of change of energy distribution after some spontaneous event.[18]

Unlike gold that won't stain or tarnish, iron, steel and concrete suffer the dragon's breath of corrosion. A century after its founding, Ryolite, Nevada's bits of broken buildings testify to the Second Law's triumph.

Mathematician Granville Sewell describes the dilemma confronting evolution when scrutinized under the laws of physics, mathematical probability and the second law.

S Steven Castro

**Shiny new cars inevitably succumb to rust and corrosion
when abandoned to the whims of mother nature.**

Forces of wind, water, snow and ice are wearing down the world's loftiest mountain chains. Grinding glaciers gouge out scenic valleys, carved midst the rocky terrain of jagged peaks, once sculpted by hydraulic action.

"The underlying principle behind the second law of thermodynamics is that natural forces do not do extremely improbable things…natural forces do not do macroscopically describable things which are extremely improbable from the microscopic point of view…

"The second law predicts that, in a closed system where only natural forces are at work, every type of order is unstable and will eventually decrease, as everything tends toward more probable (more random) states---not only will carbon and temperature distributions become more random, but the performance of all electronic devices will deteriorate, not improve.

"Natural forces, such as corrosion, erosion, fire and explosions, do not create order, they destroy it. The second law is all about probability. The reason natural forces may turn a spaceship into a pile of rubble but not vice-versa is probability: of all the possible arrangements atoms could take, only a very small percentage could fly to the moon and back." [19]

The organic world can't escape the Second Law's relentless effect.

**This Ryolite, Nevada bank lasted less than ten years.
A century later, its ruins demonstrate the Second Law's authority.**

Any 80-year-old person understands time's ravages.

Once robust and graceful twenty-year-old bodies tend to falter and bend; blotches mar once-radiant skin that dries, wrinkles, and folds; eyesight and hearing require artificial boosts; hair thins into wisps of gray while mental marbles roll in slower motion as memories falter, then fade.

Cosmetic surgery may camouflage deterioration, but an undeterred Second Law of Thermodynamics delivers the last word.

Sooner or later the all-powerful second law touches all lives on earth. Daily exercise, heavy doses of vitamins, and great genes won't prevent the most beautiful young woman or the most muscular young man from deteriorating, cell-by-cell.

Life slips into the slow lane as systems decay, drifting downhill.

Humans confronting warning signs of aging, understand the approach of their inevitable date with the grim reaper, no longer deferred by a once formidable immune system defense.

In time, the heart stops beating and black curtains shroud a cold-dust destiny. Humans can split atoms but can't create them!

Nature scoffs at Darwin's *"progress towards perfection"* cliché.

Neither man nor matter escapes the ravages of decline.

Perfection reigned at the close of creation week. But when humans fell for the great deceiver's assurance that by tasting the forbidden fruity they *"would not surely die"* but *"your eyes will be opened, and you will be like God,"* [20] devolution replaced perfection.

The Second Law of Thermodynamics, the "supreme" law of nature, erodes and ultimately shatters evolution's essence.

Wise, ancient writers addressed nature's inexorable downside trend. Citing the heavens and the foundations of the earth, the Psalmist predicted, *"they will all wear out like a garment."* [21]

V

Mother Earth's Facelift

Global Gully-Washer

"Areas of unknown extent are buried under strata which rest on them uncomformably, and could not therefore constitute the original capping, under which the whole of these rocks must once have been deeply buried…" [1]

Alfred Russell Wallace

© FloridaStock

Cathedral Rocks offer clues of nature's power.

At the beginning of creation week, Genesis describes an earth *"without form…* with darkness *"upon the face of the deep…."* [3]

Donald R. Lowe, a Stanford professor of geological and environmental sciences, with colleague Louisiana State geologist Gary R. Byerly, speculates that 3.47 years ago, earth may have been mostly covered with water when struck by a meteor. The scientists reasoned if the ocean contained the same volume of water as today, it would have been two miles deep. [4]

If true that water covered the earth prior to the creation of life, its not unreasonable to consider the possibility of a more recent worldwide hydraulic deluge covering *"all the high mountains"* after life's appearance. If earth's entire land mass were level, some guesstimate there would be enough water to inundate it's surface to a depth of several hundred feet.

A twentieth century observer believes *"the world got soaked seventy million years ago, as sea levels rose five hundred feet."* [5] The *"five hundred feet"* assessment sounds suspiciously global, at least partially reminiscent of the Genesis account of the deluge!

One of Darrow's defense witnesses in the 1925 Scopes trial avowed, *"practically all of the earth has at some time or other been covered by water."* [6] So if earth's land mass can be flooded in piecemeal fashion, why not a global gully-washer sweeping the landscape in one fell swoop?

Even Chile's Atacama Desert, reputedly the driest strip of land on the planet, is said to have been a wetlands at one time, covered with residual water from the ice age, 11,000 years before the present.

Diverse cultures perpetuate a variety of traditions describing a global hydraulic event that swept across earth's geography in ancient times. While none of these hand-me-down stories match the details spelled out in Genesis 7, the collective references tend to add credence to the occurrence of a disastrous global hydraulic event.

The secular Epic of Gilgamesh so closely parallels some highlights of the Bible's account of the global flood, some skeptics argue Moses copied portions of the Gilgamesh legend. Perhaps coincidental, the historic date assigned the Epic of Gilgamesh coincides closely with Bishop Ussher's flood chronology.

Since Moses shared a culture that descended directly from Noah through Abraham, the more rational conclusion would be that either the Gilgamesh Epic plagiarized from Noah's eyewitness record of the flood, or the 12 tablets of the Epic represent after-the-fact, multi-edited compilations of hand-me-down traditions of a very real, world-shattering event.

The Akkadian version discovered in Ashurbanipal's Ninevah library, is believed to have been dated sometime between 1,300 and 1,000 B.C. Moses, a commanding presence blessed with a giant intellect, lived and wrote before that time, preserving the primary record of the unprecedented hydraulic action in his Genesis narrative.

More than three millenniums later, Charles Darwin rejected the idea of a worldwide flood---it didn't track with his dream!

**Lacking the least shred of supporting evidence,
Darwin, the English naturalist, asserted "...*we may feel certain
...that no cataclysm has desolated the whole world.*" [7]**

We are not privy to the source of Darwin's "inside" information disputing the worldwide flood, but mountains of data suggest he didn't know what he was talking about.

While Darwin's five-year HMS Beagle adventure exposed him to exotic locations, he never came close to circumnavigating and investigating the entire   For certain he lacked credentials as either geologist or hydrologist. Nor did his five-year excursion aboard the HMS Beagle provide sufficient data for his unequivocal judgment call.

What doubter Darwin neglected to explain with his out-of-hand rejection of the Global Flood, was just how the vast coal and petroleum deposits, along with scattered cemeteries of disarticulated fossils, were discovered compacted and crushed throughout *"the whole world"* by water born sediments.

Nor did he account for the mix of land animal fossils such as the dinosaur *Muttaburrasaurus* in Australia and *T-Rex* in Canada *"found buried with marine creatures such as shellfish, turtles and fish…"* [8]

Turning his back on the Biblical account of life's creation miracle, he understood that if he bought into the deluge of Noah's day, his thesis would be hung-out-to-dry---demolished and swept away as so much fossilized flotsam in a rising tide of contrary evidence.

When it comes to the Genesis description of a hydraulic cataclysm that inundated the entire face of the planet in relatively recent times, a deluge of this magnitude chops away at the root of Darwin's tree of life.

© Wes Kime

Seventy percent of earth's surface is water covered. The remaining thirty percent is etched with watermarks! Localized floods and natural disasters have also marred and scarred that thirty percent repeatedly.

Alfred Russell Wallace, evolutionist contemporary of Darwin and hardly a fan of the global flood of Noah's day, cited *"denudation"* and *"destruction"* of the earth's geology as explanation for the lack of transitionals.

However inadvertent the reference, his description of earth's geology can be read to imply markings of a past worldwide deluge.

"…Denudation is always going on, and the rocks that we now find at the earth's surface are only a small fragment of those which were originally laid down…the frequent uncomformability of strata with those which overlie them, tell us plainly of repeated elevations and depressions of the surface, and denudation on an enormous scale.

"Almost every mountain range, with its peaks, ridges, and valleys, is but the remnant of some vast plateau eaten away by sub-aerial agencies; every range of sea-cliffs tell us of long slopes of land destroyed by the waves; while almost all the older rocks which now form the surface of the earth have been once covered with newer deposits which have long since disappeared."

Wallace opined that "…areas of unknown extent are buried under strata which rest on them uncomformably, and could not therefore, constitute the original capping under which the whole of these rocks must once have been deeply buried; because granite can only be formed, and metamorphism can only go on, deep down in the crust of the earth…

"What an overwhelming idea does this give us of the destruction of whole piles of rock, miles in thickness and covering areas comparable of those of continents…" [1]

Evolutionists and creationists agree: Mother Earth's face has undergone drastic change over time.

Waterpower's destructive revenge can still be seen two hundred miles east of Seattle where a colossal cataclysm sculpted a 16,000 square mile gouge in the earth in the blink of an eye.

Investigating geologist J. Harlan Bretz raised eyebrows when he suggested to professional peers in a 1927 lecture to the Geological Society of Washington, D.C. that the Scablands' scar didn't result from an eroding river or a grinding glacier.

His radical hypothesis that such a massive swath gouged the earth suddenly, thanks to a mega-flood, scandalized professional peers.

The listening audience of geologists dismissed the suggestion out-of-hand because it carried Biblical implications. The Bretz idea flew in the face of conventional thought committed to the idea that markings of this magnitude required millions of years of erosion by a river or a glacier.

It took time for the revolutionary Bretz interpretation to gain favor. But more than a half-century after the fact, recognition finally arrived in a ceremony tied with symbolic ribbons.

In 1980, geologists honored the aging Bretz with their highest award. [9]

The Scablands geology doesn't necessarily prove the reality of the deluge of Noah's day. It does suggest the power of a surging wall of water as high as 800 feet, released by a ruptured ice dam, can scour jagged incisions through earth's crust within a few hours.

Since gradual river erosion or glacial-paced mountains of ice are not the exclusive tools of nature for carving canyons, could it be also that a world-wide hydraulic cataclysm supplied the ice age water that cut the Scablands' swath?

When Mt. St. Helens blew its top in 1980, it cut deep gashes in the land while creating new strata layers within hours. The Scablands ice-water explosion cut its swath overnight. Neither slash took millions or even thousands of years.

Unlike the Scablands, a river runs through the heart of Arizona's Grand Canyon. Conventional theory posits that the most recent sediment layer at the surface took millions of years to accrue.

"The evolutionists' view is that a little bit of water eroded the Canyon over a long period of time through hard rock. The creationists' view is that a whole lot of water over a relatively short amount of time cut the Canyon through the still 'soft' rock layers laid down by the Flood." [10]

© Wes Kim

The Scablands scenario presents a persuasive case for hydraulic power scrambling a landscape within a few hours! The Bretz findings underscore the authority of water action in carving canyons and laying multiple sediment layers within brief moments of time.

"The average thickness of the sediments on all of the continents is approximately 1,500 meters...The average sedimentation rate measured over a period of one year is approximately 100 meters per thousand years." [11-]

Is that rate of 100 meters per millennium reasonable?

If relatively accurate, at this deposition rate all earth's sediment layers could have been put in place within 15,000 years. Not exactly a number compatible with the millions-of-years scenario.

Add a world-scale Flood to the mix and its further crunch time for landscape change resulting only from miniscule moments of gradualism.

The National Congress of Sedimentologists meeting in 1991 heard results that *"…contradict the idea of the slow build up of one layer [of sediment] followed by another. The time scale is reduced from hundreds of millions of years to one or more cataclysms producing almost instantaneous laminae.*

"These innocent-sounding words are the death knell of…the idea that the existence of thousands of meters of sediments is by itself evidence for a great age for the Earth…

Today, there are no known fossiliferous rocks forming anywhere in the world." [12]

A once pristine earth boasted a mild climate;

a carpet of lush forests; a plethora of jumbo-sized organic life forms;

and an atmosphere conducive to ecological balance.

Perfection reigned!

The Bible describes pre-flood human life extending several hundred years, even in deterioration mode. Unlike the commonly depicted, grunting, barely-human cave men, pre-flood humans, possessed knowledge to invent, to explore the world, and the wisdom to record and to preserve written accounts of events and discovery.

Defective human choice disrupted perfection, dooming the landscape.

Deterioration set in the moment the first human parents abused their freedom in ego-driven pursuit of faux "wisdom." Since that springtime of life, precipitous ecological decline followed, engulfing the natural world.

Eventually, nature's eco-skid was marked by the hydraulic cataclysm that unleashed *"the floodgates of heaven"* [13] in an unrelenting downpour that raged, non-stop, for forty days and nights. When *"…all the springs of the great deep burst forth"* [13] to mix with 960 hours of heaven's open floodgates, the planet succumbed to devastating upheaval.

© Andrly Nekrasov

After forty days of pounding terror, *"all the high mountains under the heavens were covered…to a depth of more than twenty feet."* [13] The water inundation was aided and abetted by *"a wind over the earth,"* [14] unleashing Tsunami-like mountains of churning waves.

Before the torrent of destruction was complete, hurricane force winds added to the raging fury, shredding earth's crust like a bolt of sheer cloth.

Perfection disappeared.

While much pre-flood knowledge would have been lost in the destructive waters of the deluge, the eight survivors would logically have preserved critical, encyclopedic information much as families today save heirlooms from a fire.

If Noah, and his family, had used this narrow slice of time to record the drama of the most harrowing experience of their lives, preserved in written form, along with descriptions of the pre-flood world, the prized, museum quality records would have been passed to future generations.

Moses, author of Genesis, would have had access to much of this data available through his royal education in Egypt and his unique cultural heritage.

The deluge event was far more significant than the ruthless rampage of an angry nature---it exposes the sorry state of the human race. The exceptional longevity of pre-flood humankind only enhanced an already tainted environment where evil's contagion flourished.

© poutnik

Devil's Tower, remnant of a volcanic plug.

While the *"heroes of old"* were *"men of renown,"* they had become so prone to *"violence"* and degradation, that *"all people on earth had corrupted their ways"* and *"every inclination of the thoughts of his heart was only evil all the time."* [15]

The Lord was *"grieved…and His heart was filled with pain"* when He *"saw how great man's wickedness on the earth had become…So the Lord said, 'I will wipe mankind, whom I have created, from the face of the earth."* [15]

Taking God at His word, the meager traces of human beings in the fossil record is not due to some haphazard evolutionary process, but rather the catastrophic hydraulic event that not only buried coal beds and oil fields but also wiped out mankind's pre-flood existence.

No wonder, *"the fossils that decorate our family tree are so scarce that there are still more scientists than specimens…all the physical evidence we have for human evolution can still be placed, with room to spare, inside a single coffin."* [17]

Nothing remotely comparable to the global flood occurs today! The hydraulic action that scoured earth's face with catastrophic death and destruction was a one-time event.

©Yurly Kulyk

*"I have set my rainbow in the clouds, and
it will be a sign of the covenant between me and the earth."* [16]

The Flood alone didn't complete Mother Earth's facelift!

After the days of Noah, nature's arsenal has demonstrated repeatedly its devastating power by unleashing multiple destructive forces that are fearsome but something less than worldwide.

Localized floods, earthquakes, tectonic plate shifts, volcanic explosions, radical climate swings, the erosive power of hurricane winds, and the relentless grind of ocean tides have cut swaths and carved stone monuments.

Tsunamis erase coastal villages, trigger fires resulting from natural gas explosions, and threaten all forms of life with terrorizing doses of radioactivity released by earthquake and water damage to vulnerable atomic power plants.

But never again will there be another global scale deluge!

"Whenever the rainbow appears in the clouds, I will wee it and remember the everlasting covenant between God and all living creatures of every kind on the earth." [18]

VI

Tracking the Perfect Cataclysm

Fossil Residue

"Some kinds of catastrophic action is nearly always necessary
for the burial and preservation of fossils. Nothing comparable to the
tremendous fossiliferous beds of fish, mammals, reptiles…that are found
in many places around the world is being formed today." [1]
John C. Whitcomb and Henry M. Morris

© Kavram

**Meandering ribbons of water, like this horseshoe bend
in the Colorado River, display colorful canyon cuts
preserving subtle clues to deep time.**

A treasure chest of 20,000 fossils has been discovered buried fifty feet below the surface of a southwestern China mountain.

A team of *"scientists led by Shixue Hu of the Chengdu Geological Center detailed their findings online Dec. 22 [2010] in the journal Proceedings of the Royal Society B."* The cache includes *"exceptionally well preserved"* fossils *"with more than half of them completely intact, including soft tissues."* [2]

The presence of *"fossil land plants suggest the marine community lived near a conifer forest"* in a *"tropical climate."* [2]

The Permian mass extinction event, conventionally dated at 251.4 million years before the present, took out a majority of insects, an estimated 70% of terrestrial vertebrates and a staggering 96% of marine life. Even with sudden burial from catastrophic hydraulic action preventing early decay, *"soft tissues"* could not have survived for millions of years.

Extinctions were not solely the by-product of the failure of some ancient species to compete for survival and to transmit its *"unaltered likeness"* to some *"distant futurity descendant."*

Prime candidate for across-the-board extinctions of plant and animal life is the hydraulic powered event depicted in Genesis that tore apart an entire ecosystem. Dry land succumbed to an unprecedented water inundation wreaking environmental havoc. Species extinction and ecological decline remain the cataclysm's legacy!

Sudden inundation by water-borne sediment wiped out entire species creating jumbled masses of disarticulated fossil bones, jammed together in fossil graveyards. This evidence correlates comfortably with the Genesis narrative of a relatively recent global gully-washer where water-powered devastation rearranged mountains of terrain delivering indiscriminate collateral damage. Remnants of cataclysmic intrusion pervade dry land masses. Residual fossils provide clues to original biodiversity.

Another treasure-trove of tiny fossil embryos discovered in China were *"…most likely buried alive one day in a sudden catastrophic overflow of sediment."* [3] Absent such a process, dead organic material, exposed to the surface, will decay naturally and disappear.

Marine life relics of pre-history have been discovered strewn across landmasses thousands of feet above sea level on the slopes of the Andes and the Himalayas, far from present day oceans.

"Fossilized dinosaur tracks scale sheer mountain cliffs, which are tilted topsy-turvy by some unseen, latent power—trademark testimony to the magnitude of cataclysmic force. Seashells and fossilized marine life litter bone-dry hilltops and mountain slopes, far above today's sea level.

"Chains of today's high-altitude, rugged terrain lay submerged underwater in the past, until sea beds awash in the currents of a cataclysmic deluge or powered by some convulsive thrust inside the Earth's crust pushed mountains skyward from the ocean's floor." [4]

The Siwaliks, foothills to the Himalayas, which run for several hundred miles and are 2,000 to 3,000 feet high *"…contain extraordinarily rich beds crammed with fossils: hundreds of feet of sediment, packed with the jumbled bones of scores of extinct species…the remains of terrestrial animals, not marine creatures."* [5]

"A fossil fish has been unearthed 17,000 feet up the slopes of the Andes and marine fossil limestone has been spotted in the Himalayas at an altitude of 20,000 feet!

"Marine fossils are found on top of glacial deposits as in the case of the whale skeletons…covering glacial deposits in Michigan…Whale fossils have also been found 440 feet above sea level north of Lake Ontario; more than 500 feet above sea level in Vermont; and some 600 feet above sea level in the Montreal area." [6]

The fossil bones of a whale were discovered on a desert hilltop near Bakersfield, California. Sea going creatures didn't simply crawl or swim up the mountains to die but are residual clues to a past natural disaster that gave Mother Nature a major league facelift.

With or without a villain meteorite killing off an entire species, it was sudden hydraulic action that fossilized Gobi dinosaurs. At the time it was a wetter and greener Gobi and home to *"…hundreds of dinosaurs and mammals…Avalanches of water-soaked sand buried the animals alive, creating one of the world's richest fossil sites.*

"The fossils appear remarkably complete in that…all the bones are connected to form whole skeleton…death was sudden, and the ill-fated creatures were quickly buried before scavenging animals could make off with the meaty bits." [7]

Thousands of fossil dinosaur eggs have been discovered strewn across a parched square mile of layered mudstone within the Argentine badlands at the Auca Mahuevo site.

"Every evidence shows that the embryos may have perished in a flood that quickly buried the eggs in a layer of silt and mud. This made it possible for the soft tissues to fossilize before decaying, an extremely rare occurrence." [8]

Irrespective of conjectured time frames, *"dinosaur bones…had to fall into water and be buried to be preserved, and most dinosaurs spent most of their time on dry land."* [9]

Mineshafts honeycombing through thousands of feet of West Virginia's mountainous terrain, lead to a black, biomass treasure that heats homes and generates electricity. Twenty-nine West Virginia miners lost their lives in April, 2010, while extracting coal from those underground tunnels that extend five-miles beneath the light of day.

Masses of compressed ferns and trees, a residue of another time, provide the raw material for those rich veins of coal several hundred feet deep. A once lush band of living vegetation, thriving under the sun's rays, didn't die a natural death. Coal didn't just bury itself but remains a visible footprint, left by a colossal hydraulic event that moved and built mountains. Mother Earth underwent an unprecedented face-lift that shifted millions of tons of terra firma, crushing and creating the biomass mined as coal.

Conventional time frames postulate a long and tedious process for forming the strata housing fossil fuels.

Is a multi-million-year process realistic?

Coal bed excavations raise doubts!

Take another look at the mega-tons of rocky terrain piled thousands-of-feet deep atop coal beds! Conventional traditions centered on evolution's gradualism leave questions hanging, ignored and unanswered.

Where did this mountainous stack of stone originate?

How did it arrive in place to pile on and bury the biomass?

What source of power shuffled the mega loads of sediment?

Why isn't comparable action taking place today?

Fossil remains of trees have been discovered embedded upright in coal seams with vertical trunks pointing skyward, penetrating through multiple coal seam layers. This polystrate tree phenomenon argues for sudden and near-simultaneous burial of multi-layered strata, poses a time quandary not resolved by multi-million-year scenarios.

"Polystrate trees are fossil trees that extend through several layers of strata, often twenty feet or more in length. There is no doubt that this type of fossil was formed relatively quickly; otherwise it would have decomposed while waiting for strata to slowly accumulate around it." [10]

The remains of plants and animals stranded on earth's surface, exposed to nature's ravages, will decay and disappear. Gradual decay won't do it. But that same organic matter can provide the raw material for fossil fuels if buried suddenly, pressured by tons of sediment, deprived of oxygen, and subjected to heat. [11]

Peat bogs can't do it; peat has root systems, coal beds do not.

The multi-hued fossil trees highlighting this barren landscape were
once part of a flourishing forest before being swept away
by cascading water.

A slice of a petrified tree from Arizona's Petrified Forest,
destroyed in the path of an ancient flood.

So when and how did this prodigious wealth of lush vegetation and animal life find itself buried in Mother Earth? A global-scale, catastrophic Flood stands out as the most reasonable explanation.

Commerce rides wheels greased by non-renewable, biomass resources pumped 24/7 from hard-to-find hiding places. The world's largest supply of crude oil was discovered in 1938, 4,247 feet below the sands of the Saudi Arabian desert. [12]

But once tapped and pumped dry, the pools of black gold treasure are gone for good. Civilization's voracious fuel consumption collides with sober reality---production of oil and natural gas liquids peaked in 1970. [13]

© Warren L. Johns

Maryland's East/West bound Interstate #68 slices through a cross-section of breathtaking geology. Folded sediment would likely have been damp when bent into strata's colorful curves.

Not only does Rocky Gap strata shelter a rainbow of earth tone colors, it also presents graceful arches of folded strata that could have hardened only after folding. Enormous pressure must have shifted giant chunks of still damp sediments carving arced designs in the strata when solidified.

A raging force of destructive events,

acting in unison while ravaging the face of Mother Earth,

could qualify as the all-time "Perfect Cataclysm."

Volcanic explosions, meteorite impacts, hurricane force winds, earthquakes, tectonic shifts, valleys chiseled by glaciers, shifting magnetic poles, drastic climate changes, radical extinctions of plant and animal life forms, and rampaging water are not uncommon single events.

Earth's inorganic land and sea mass coalesce in a kaleidoscope of constant change, powered by the planet's internal heat engine, pushing to the surface, building a dynamic ecosystem stage.

If those natural forces were unleashed more or less simultaneously as a package deal, worldwide, the magnitude of destruction would be unprecedented during the most recent 4,000 years of earth's history.

Earlier, something approximating that radical package happened!

When *"all the springs of the great deep"* burst, volcanic raging ovens spewing mega tons of dust into the atmosphere would upset world climates!

Krakatoa exploded August 23, 1883 snuffing out 36,000 human lives while hurling ocean waves as high as fifty. The twenty billion cubic meters of ash and debris blown more than 20 miles into the global stratosphere caused temperatures to drop by ten percent during the next three years, impacting climates as far distant as Europe. [14]

With a force estimated at thirty times that of Mount St. Helens, Alaska's Novarupta erupted on June 6, 1912, polluting the sky with a mantle of gaseous fumes and ash while lowering worldwide temperatures by as much as two degrees. [15]

In what is now the "Yellowstone caldera," the scene of at least three super volcano explosions in the past, the most sever is believed to have been *"a thousand times the size of the Mount Helens eruption in 1980."* [16]

"…Ocean temperature at the end of the Genesis Flood was likely as warm as 100⁰ F or more. Such a warm ocean would be an explanation for the Ice Age because of the excessive evaporation of water into the atmosphere and deposition of snow in the polar regions and on mountaintops that would have occurred.

"An ocean with a SST [sea surface temperature] equal to or greater than 100°F would also likely have produced large frequencies and intensities of hurricanes beyond anything experienced today.

"…Giant hurricanes called hyper canes would likely have occurred over major portions of the earth. They would have grown to hundreds of miles in diameter, produced horizontal winds of over 300 miles per hour, had vertical winds of 100 miles per hour, and precipitated rain at rates greater than 10 inches per hour.

"Large amounts of erosion of the unconsolidated sediments would have occurred on the continents following the Flood. In this context, today's increasing hurricane activity represents a minor oscillation in the steady-state condition at the end of about 5,000 years of cooling." [17]

"…The abundant layers of lava and ash, mixed with sedimentary rocks around the world, attest to extensive volcanism during the flood…Requirements for an ice age are a combination of much cooler summers and greater snowfall than in today's climate. …Volcanic dust and aerosols remaining in the atmosphere following the Flood" [18]

The dust residue from Tambora's 1815 eruption upset climates 10,000 miles distant in New England, parts of Canada and Europe. 1816 was dubbed *"the year without a summer"* when an *"unprecedented series of cold snaps chilled the area. Heavy snow fell in June, and frost caused crop failures in July and August. Sea ice was extensive in Hudson Bay and Davis Strait…"* [19]

"What happened to bring on a cataclysm so widespread and abrupt?

"The answer smoldered 10,000 miles away, in today's Indonesia…the 13,000-foot volcano Tambora erupted on an island near Java. For a week thunderous explosions rocked the region and were heard a thousand miles away. Fiery ejections of rock, flame, gas, and steam shot into the stratosphere.

"Thirty-six cubic miles of earth blasted heavenward-the greatest release of energy ever known, dwarfing a nuclear explosion and even a nuclear war. At week's end 12,000 Javanese lay dead, tsunamis had killed thousands more on distant islands, and the volcano stood a mile shorter than before.

"The trillions of tons of material that Tambora shot into the atmosphere circled the earth with the winds. For more than a year they blocked sunlight from the northern hemisphere, dimming the planet with that 'sable hue.' " [20]

So what happened to excess water left from the cataclysm that devoured the earth?

Did the wind sent to dry the Flood's waters contribute to the quick-freeze that introduced vast sheets of ice and an ice age, so bitterly frigid, that thousands of years later, parts of the planet are still clamped in its grip?

Could the Global Flood's residue be the primary source of ice-age water or the glacier that buried Manhattan Island to a depth of 300 feet?

The impact of volcanic ash on the global climate combined with the unprecedented magnitude of residual Flood water make prime suspects responsible for the steep temperature drop that activated a freezing climate.

Antarctica, Greenland, and the Arctic bear immense burdens of frozen water. One estimate suggests the ice and snow saturating the surfaces of Greenland and Antarctica together contain 70% of the planet's fresh water.

Snow masses still cap the poles and crown mountain ranges. Sea-bound glaciers creep slowly down craggy mountain slopes, feeding thirsty oceans that can sculpt shorelines.

"Perhaps as much as 95% of the ice near the poles could have accumulated in the first 500 years or so after the Flood…

"The 'annual' layers deep in the Greenland ice sheet may be related to individual storms rather than seasonal accumulations...

"Calculations of the number of layers laid down assuming the ice sheet accumulated rapidly near the bottom show that as many as 100 storms may have swept the polar regions each year accompanied by frequent volcanic eruptions." [21]

With ice layers towering three miles deep in some places and 90% of the earth's ice crowning Antarctica's land base, it's thought provoking that *"Three hundred miles (500 km) from the South Pole, sandstone beds lined with coal deposits…laid down in marshy conditions under a cool, moist climate"* and that *"fossil leaves and wood found in Antarctica indicate it was once warmer and forested."* [22]

Greenland's ice sheet, *"roughly the size of Mexico,"* covers 80% of its surface. In 2005, its *"glaciers discharged more than twice as much ice as they did in 1996…enough fresh water to supply Los Angeles for 220 years."* [23]

In the event the frozen water storage plants of Antarctica and Greenland should feel the heat of global warming and melt entirely, ocean levels could rise an estimated 230 feet!

Then there are tsunamis!

A balmy, after-Christmas Sunday morning, December 26, 2004, started like all previous holidays in Southeast Asia's favorite get-a-ways. Holiday celebrants basked beachside in the tropical breezes that bathed resorts lining the shores of the Indian Ocean. Until this moment, the "Tsunami" label existed outside the common vocabulary of most tourists.

But nature, sometimes a cruel teacher, delivered a crash course in demonstrating the unimaginable havoc possible from an undersea earthquake carrying a force equal to hundreds of atomic explosions.

With little advance awareness, an angry ocean, generating waves surging at speeds up to 500 miles-per-hour, swept aside all in its path.

The grim reaper's scythe cut a swath through ocean shores in Tanzania, Kenya, Somalia, Seychelles, Maldives, India, Bangladesh, Burma, Sri Lanka, Indonesia, Thailand, and Malaysia. The lives of an estimated 175,000 plus victims were snuffed out by an all-consuming ocean stoked by a Richter Scale 9.0 earthquake epicentered off the coast of Sumatra.

© Diana Lundin

**Yosemite's Half-Dome, a silent sentinel to antiquity,
marks the relentless march of time and the trail of a glacier
that eroded its front half while tracing a trail through the valley.**

The impact shifted the geographic foundation of one Indonesian island. A piece of the ocean floor more than 700 miles long (distance between Denver and Chicago) and 10 miles wide jolted 100 feet upward unleashing 135 cubic miles of churning water.

The magnitude of the destruction removed entire towns and left battered human remains mixed with the debris of civilization strewn helter-skelter in grotesque heaps.

The ripple effect stretched ugly tentacles westward 3,750 miles to the east coast of Africa snuffing out the lives of 298 Somalians in the coastal village of Foar. The initial crushing onslaught, ripped seashore lobster beds, depositing a harvest of death high up the slopes of adjacent hills. [24]

An angry Mother Nature wasn't through.

The tsunami nightmare swept Japan's shores March 11, 2011, triggered by another 9.0 Richter scale earthquake that shook the foundations of the nation. Shattering homes and shifting earth's axis, the power of this killer jolt pushed the nation's main island eight feet farther to the east.

Showers of deadly radiation soon followed, released by ruptured components of vulnerable seacoast atomic power plants, directly in the eye of the storm.

When the *"fountains of the deep"* exploded, smashed tectonic plates would have broken land masses into continent-sized pieces of a ragged jig-saw puzzle, disrupting magnetic fields, scattering toxic clouds of climate-altering volcanic dust, and sending portions of earth's water blanket into deep-freeze mode.

Those same, colliding tectonic plates, larded with fossil-bound remains of marine creatures, also could propel jagged mountain ranges skyward where oxygen was thin and temperatures cold.

Consider the effect of combining the Flood's roaring hydraulic turbulence, storm surges, rogue waves with the shake, rattle, and roll of multiple, magnitude nine plus earthquakes.

Then, blend in multiples of Indian and Pacific Ocean style tsunamis.

Finally, add a gargantuan cosmic discordance with a shower of meteorites cutting 120-mile wide craters as happened once in the seabed off Mexico's Yucatan Peninsula. [25]

Ironically, some who accept the feasibility of earth's entire dinosaur population being destroyed by a meteor exploding off the Yucatan, reject a global flood that sabotaged primal perfection, diminished eco diversity, extinguished a broad spectrum of plant and animal life while scrambling land surfaces, leaving them unrecognizable.

Multiple natural disasters have scarred earth's face.

No single destructive event compares to the ferocious cataclysm that swept life away more than 4,000 years before the present.

Darwin (1809-1872) didn't live contemporaneously with Noah. Nor did he offer convincing evidence supporting his assertion that *"no cataclysm has desolated the whole world."*

His unsupported personal bias is pitted against a vivid, detailed account of a cataclysmic global flood written several thousand years nearer to the event than when he wrote his opinion. His rush to judgment, denying a worldwide flood, leaves hanging a batch of questions!

Can giant-sized dinosaurs form fossils if covered gradually, at a minuscule rate, when preservation requires prompt and complete burial with multiple tons of sediment to avoid decay?

How can mass burials that created fossil cemeteries be explained apart from the churning force of hydraulic energy?

How could billions of barrels of petroleum and mega tons of coal form without submersion of flora, overwhelmed by the sudden surge of sediment-laden water?

What rationale other than hydraulic catastrophe better accounts for the preservation of any fossil residue of any former plant or animal life?

Man Hunt

Human Genealogy

"Is its explanatory power any more than verbal?

…Evolution not only conveys no knowledge, but seems somehow to convey anti-

knowledge, apparent knowledge which is actually harmful to systematics…" [1]

Colin Patterson

"Jesus loves the little children, All the children of the world,
Red and yellow, black and white,
All are precious in His sight,
Jesus loves the little children of the world."

On May 19, 2009, the fossil "Ida" was introduced to the world as *"the scientific equivalent of the Holy Grail."*[3] Split from a block of shale by amateurs in 1983, the lemur-like Ida measured a meager 50 or so centimeters from head-to-tip-of-tale

Under the auspices of New York's prestigious American Museum of Natural History, one enthusiastic sponsor glowed that the Ida fossil *"will probably be the one that will be pictured in all textbooks for the next 100 years."*[3]

Another optimist declared Ida to be *"the eighth wonder of the world,"* noting *"we're not dealing with our grand-grand-grandmother, but perhaps with our grand, grand, grandaunt."*[3]

A Princeton paleontologist discounted skeptics by welcoming the alleged 47-million-year-old fossil as *"almost certainly part of the lineage that led to monkey, apes and humans."*[4]

Still, Ida's auspicious introduction *"as the eighth wonder of the world"* didn't last long. Her fifteen-minutes of fame passed into oblivion abruptly, making way for "Ardi," another female fossil, destined to steal Ida's crown!

Unearthed in 1994, *"it took a multidisciplinary team 15 years to excavate Ardi, digitally remove distortions, and analyze her bones."*[5]

Ardi's resume included the claim she lived 4.4 million years before the present---one million years before the date previously assigned to the still famous Lucy.

One-hundred-twenty-five residue scraps of Ardi's fossil bones, were pieced together with the help of computer technology. The composite result resembled a four-foot tall female ape, with *"a body and brain only slightly larger than a chimpanzee."* [5]

Capable of walking on two legs, Ardi's feet displayed a long, oblique-angled, *"opposable big toe,"* [5] facilitating tree navigation.

It took scientists mere months to conclude *"the 47-million-year-old fossil of the early primate called Ida…is not a direct ancestor to humans, as initially claimed during her debut this year."* [5]

As to Ardi, *"not all paleoanthropologists are convinced that Ar. ramidus was our ancestor or even a hominin."* [5]

Does believed ability to stand erect necessarily equate "biped" status? Or qualify for sharing common ancestry with humans?

Evolution once relied on primitive paleontology's fossil bone fragments to conjecture linkage. Bone cemeteries can't do it!

Microbiology science looks beyond bones to DNA.

Without clear-cut evidence of a long series of mutated DNA strings to corroborate evolution's postulated transitions, positive proof of Lucy's, Ida's or Ardi's imagined link to humans is wishful thinking!

Darwin never met Ardi, Lucy or Ida.

He advised humans should not *"feel ashamed"*

of common descent from *"Old World division"* monkeys.

After devising a theory built on *"chance,"* Darwin refused to acknowledge *"Design"* in nature, while admitting to Harvard professor Asa Gray, he found himself *" in an utterly hopeless muddle."* [6]

In a culture proud of its ancestry and revered heraldry, evolution's champion diminished his own family's roots by claiming linkage to a long organic chain of life beginning with that accidental appearance of a first living cell derived from non-living matter.

In an in-your-face dogma of contempt, and without benefit of persuasive evidence, godless theory mocks the creation miracle, alleging *Homo sapiens* represent nothing more than mutant descendants from an unknown ancient fish sharing ancestry with *"Old world division"* monkeys.

© Rissa Lee Johns

If an evolutionist told these kids they descended from a fish ancestor, they would laugh, thinking it a joke.

The ancestral chain envisioned by Darwin linking man-to-molecule, by accidental luck-of-the-draw, defies reason. Such abstract linkage arouses skepticism---particularly so when incorporating a fantasy "fish story!"

The philosopher/naturalist jump-starts the make-believe process, by blazing a non-existent, transitional trail of organic continuity *"through a long line of diversified forms"* beginning with *"higher mammals …derived from an ancient marsupial "* then latching onto *"some reptile-like or some amphibian-like creature."* [7]

With imagination unchecked, Darwin linked human genealogy to an unknown, pre-historic sea creature, asserting *"all the members of the vertebrate kingdom are derived from some fish-like animal."* [8] In his opinion, *"Man is the co-descendant with other mammals of a common progenitor."* [9]

Evolution's patron saint plunged ahead on a genealogical roll, saddling his own and mankind's family tree with yet another mysterious ancestor, envisioned as neither male nor female.

"The early progenitor of all the Vertebrata must have been an aquatic animal, provided with branchiae, with the two sexes united in the same individual…." [10] *"Some extremely remote progenitor of the whole vertebrate kingdom appears to have been hermaphrodite or androgynous."* [11]

He assumed *"the progenitors of man must have been aquatic in their habits; for morphology plainly tells us that our lungs consist of a modified swim-bladder…the heart existed as a simple pulsating vessel."* [11]

Darwin conjured-up man as having *"descended from a hairy quadruped …probably arboreal in its habits."* [12]

Waxing eloquent, he insisted, *"early progenitors of man were no doubt once covered with hair, both sexes having beards; their ears were pointed and capable of movement; and their bodies were provided with a tail."* [13]

The linkage of successor life forms resulting from Darwin's postulated organic chain of physical traits, acquired by gradual use or disuse of body parts, over multi-millions of years, doesn't warrant feature recognition in human family photo albums.

The faces of Aunts "Lucy," "Ida" or "Ardi" are nowhere to be seen.

If Darwin's words are taken at face value, man's surmised ancestral linkage translates roughly: *"…fish-like animal…aquatic animal…reptile-like…ancient marsupial…hairy quadruped…arboreal in its habits…sexes united in same individual… hermaphrodite or androgynous… covered with hair…both sexes having beards…ears were pointed, capable of movement …higher mammals…"*

Darwin floats this breath-taking rhetoric despite the reality this genealogical zoo of organic life forms leading to and eventually linking *"Old World division"* monkeys with humans, doesn't exist!

While not a highly visible admission printed in one of his published tomes, Darwin admitted privately in a letter to Asa Gray, *"…I am quite conscious that my speculations run beyond the bounds of true science."* [14]

He might well have said, far *"beyond!"*

Born to a cocoon of wealth and social status in a nineteenth-century British society with fiercely defined classes, Charles Darwin reflected a jaundiced view of life outside his circle of privilege. He wrapped his doctrine around a bias of narrow, social perspective.

He pictured himself and his male compatriots as mankind's fittest, surveying life from the peak of the heap, superior beneficiaries of the monkey-to-man scenario, leading the human race ever farther away from their alleged *"arboreal"* [12] roots.

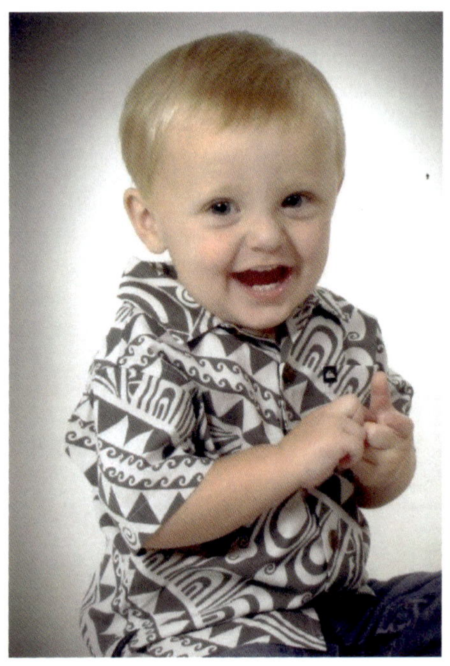 

Human genealogy does not share common ancestry with apes or monkeys. All humans have been designed and created, *sui generis*, in the image of God.

Cross sections of Darwin's unvarnished pronouncements raise twenty-first century eyebrows. Condescending prejudices infect his declarations! Consider this cross-section of discredited thought!

"…Man has…become superior to woman." [15] *"The average standard of mental power in man must be above that of a woman."* [16]

Darwin's imagined tree of life, is an imaginary withered stick, bereft of leaves, branches or roots.

Darwin's *"arboreal"* assertion set the stage for the conjectured family tree descending from some grand pappy, monkey-type critter. Without a hint of equivocation, he attempted to pin-the-tale on the unsuspecting monkey for the entire human family.

He described the Simiadae as an *"Old World division …after these had diverged from the New World division."* [20] He revealed the Simiadaes had *"branched off into two great stems; the New World and Old World monkeys; and from the latter, at a remote period, Man, the wonder and glory of the Universe proceeded…"* [22]

To minimize the shock value from this news impacting the considerable pride of peers, he encouraged followers to hold their heads high, assuring, *"…we may, with our present knowledge, approximately recognize our heritage; nor need we feel ashamed of it…"* [21]

Perhaps Darwin wasn't *"ashamed"* of the monkey swinging from his own family's woodwork, but his pointed portrayal of this presumed predecessor posing as some ancient great-grand-parent might not so easily have passed scrutiny when viewed through the discriminating lens of a Victorian family's tradition.

Creationists may agree that humans deserve recognition as *"the wonder and glory of the Universe,"* [21] while rejecting the dubious idea of life's accidental origin in some *"little warm pond"* followed by a tortured trail of transitionals climbing relentlessly up the taxonomic chart to this prestigious pinnacle.

Has anyone heard even the most devout evolutionist boast of a scaly-skinned, grand pappy Pisces, spawned in the briny deep or a hairy, ape-type ancestor noted for tree-swinging talents?

This sorry fiction doesn't make the cut!

Fact is, neither monkeys nor fish have anything to do with any human family tree---including Charles Darwin's.

The same guy who saw no need to hang heads in embarrassment as to common blood lines with ape-like ancestry betrayed personal blindness to racism, going out of his way to look down his nose figuratively on human races he defined as *"savage."*

After leading readers all the way from primordial slime to the arboreal swing set, Darwin found a place for man parading from the *"barbarian"* or *"savage state"* onward to *"lower races"* and supposedly upward to *"men of a superior class,"* [22] a position reserved to the socially elite, dominating Europe's nineteenth-century.

Alexander Stephens, vice president of the short-lived Confederate States of America, couldn't have agreed more.

In his 1861 "Cornerstone Speech," attempting to justify *"the immediate cause of the late rupture and present revolution,"* the arrogant politician preached racial superiority as moral justification for slavery.

"Our new Government is founded upon…the great truth that the negro is not equal to the white man; that slavery, subordination to the superior race, is his natural and moral condition." [23]

Unscientific political propaganda! Pitifully ignorant! The American Civil War blood bath, fostered by blatant racism, snuffed out 620,000 lives.

Ever since Darwin conjectured man's divergence from *"Old World division"* monkeys, paleoanthropologists have scrambled, combing strata, looking for non-existent corroborating clues.

Monkeys, bonobos and apes populate the African jungle scene but would be rarities in European or Middle Eastern landscapes. It comes as no surprise that Darwinists seek monkey/human common ancestry evidence where knuckle-dragging primate populations roam.

Hence, the "out of Africa" scenario---an implicit imperative corollary to the human/ape common ancestry debacle!

Speculation suggests an "out-of-Africa" migration began 200,000 years before the present. This leaves a 150,000-year time gap until 50,000 years ago when the Middle East appears to be the geographic hub of population migration. [25]

Questions arise as to the validity of conventional time frames as well as to the suggestion early human migration took place "out-of-Africa" rather than "into Africa" from the Middle East! A significant blow to the "out-of-Africa" tradition is a recent claim that fossil evidence shows *"anthropoid apes colonized Africa 39 million years ago rather than evolving there."*[26]

Another snag in the out-of-Africa idea comes from a cave in China where *"bones 60,000 years older than previous finds present 'a strong challenge' to the out-of-Africa theory and the 'traditional early-human time line.'"* [27]

Given the human genetic traces emanating in most directions from the Middle East migration hub, a strong argument can be made that human migration routes led "into Africa" and "into Asia" rather than "out-of-Africa," despite the upset risk to Darwin's monkey-to-man conjecture.

After years of combing vast ranges of African turf, pitifully few bits and pieces of fossil bones, even arguably categorized as pre-human, have turned up.   The clearly human Hofmeyr Skull, discovered in South Africa in the twentieth century, has been conventionally dated at 36,000 years before the present. [28]

But since conventional dating suggests migrations from the Middle East in multi-directions to all points on the compass occurred 50,000 years BP, "Mr. Hofmeyr" might just as readily support "into Africa" theory as "out-of-Africa" thinking.

Studio Six

**These three young women will never be convinced
they descended from some ancestor fish.**

Before swallowing the allocated conventional dating of 36,000, 50,000 or 200,000 years before the present, the Hofmeyr Skull deserves a closer look.

Mr. Hofmeyr's age was determined *"by measuring the amount of radiation that had been absorbed by sand grains that filled the inside of the skull's braincase."* [28]

While initially this assessment may sound respectable, the troubling question lingers: Does the calculated date of Hofmeyer's burial necessarily match the date of the surrounding burial site turf?

Without contrary evidence, could Hofmeyr arguably have walked the earth as recently as 4,000 or 5,000 years before the present?

As to Neanderthals, Bible scholars speculate as to whether the oversized *Nephilim* race of Genesis 6:4 and Numbers 13:33 could account for the Neanderthal fossils?

However tempting the correlation, the speculative question rests on the table, unanswered.

**Unable to identify evolution in action in the living world,
a roster of brazen frauds and phonies have attempted to
"salt the mine" with make-believe fossil evidence.**

Perhaps frustrated by the shortfall of evidence supporting evolution theory attempting to link human ancestry to unrelated animal species, blatant fraud took the stage. A weird parade of concocted "missing links," provides comic relief but does nothing to enhance Darwinian theory!

"Nebraska Man," purposed to be one million years old, grabbed 1922 headlines until exposed as nothing more than a single tooth of an extinct pig. "Ramapithecus" also missed the cut as an alleged "missing link" ancestor to *Homo sapiens* when ultimately identified as nothing more than an extinct orangutan.

But the prize for arrogant deceit goes to the fabricators of the so-called but never-was, "Piltdown Man."

In 1912, Charles Dawson, British lawyer and amateur fossil connoisseur, rose to the challenge, proclaiming his "discovery" of the fossil remains of Piltdown Man. The fraudulent bone scrap claimed cache as an ancient fossil tying apes and *Homo sapiens* to a common ancestry.

News of the find sent shivers of satisfaction down the spines of Darwin aficionados. The artfully darkened fossil skull and jaw shamelessly shouted "transitional"---the long sought fruition of Darwin's unverified dream!

The Piltdown fraud fabricator had pieced together a modern human skull with the jaw bone of an ape, then stained the monstrosity to mimic the appearance of antiquity. The faked "evidence" was then planted in an English gravel pit in prep for its orchestrated "discovery."

Evolutionists recognized as respected scientists swallowed the bait!

The ballyhooed "fossil" remains were promptly "authenticated" and awarded a place of honor in the British Museum.

By the time Attorney Clarence Darrow took on the Scopes defense in Tennessee's 1925 "monkey trial," Piltdown's credentials reflected enshrinement in evolution's citadel of "fact." [29]

In a written filing for the defense, University of Chicago Anthropologist, Dr. Fay Cooper-Cole, added his voice to the chorus preaching admiration for the find.

Both Darrow and his expert witness had been hoodwinked, conned by the infectious ballyhoo touting egregious deceit. They bit on the phony discovery by cluttering the trial's record with written quotes classifying Piltdown Man as *"…distinctly human…an approach toward man in very ancient strata…*

"…The crushed skull of a woman and a skull can scarcely be distinguished from that of a chimpanzee…The skull is exceedingly thick and its capacity much less than a modern man, but it is distinctly human, while, as indicated, the jaw approaches that of an anthropoid. Here again we seem to have an approach toward man in very ancient strata." [30]

The celebrated defense counsel further buttressed his case by introducing citations from the 1914 edition of George W. Hunter's *Civic Biology*, the textbook then in use in Dayton, Tennessee's science classrooms.

The text overflowed with patently racist, survival of the fittest mentality---the kind of virus that infected Hitler's Germany in the 1930's.

Ugly, unscientific garbage, glared ominously from pages 195-6 of the despicably flawed volume.

"There is a greater difference between the lowest type of monkey and the highest type of ape than there is between the highest type of ape and the lowest savage…Undoubtedly there once lived upon the earth races of men who were much lower in their mental organization than the present inhabitants…we find that at first he must have been little better than one of the lower animals…

"At the present time there exist upon the earth five races or varieties of man, each different from the other in instincts, social customs, and, to an extent, in structure…the highest type of all, the Caucasians, represented by the civilized white inhabitants of Europe and America." [31]

Hunter's *Civic Biology* has long since been discarded, out-of-print, but not before corrupting young minds with toxic fraud.

Piltdown Man cheated "death" for an extended time, flummoxing evolutionists for nearly half the twentieth century.

Mr. Piltdown thrived as scientific "gospel" for forty-one years. It took until November 21, 1953, for the much-hyped patchwork of old bones to be exposed as bald-faced fraud---the year DNA's double-helix design burst onto the stage, revolutionizing genomic science.

Evolution's curious quest to confirm molecule-to-monkey-to-man remains unconfirmed---one or more bubbles out of plumb. The human genome defies the concept.

Mendel's law of genetics applies to all living organisms, including humans. Mendel's law and evolution theory are mutually exclusive.

The human body consists of an estimated fifty trillion cells composed of ten million atoms each. The DNA of a single cell comes packed reportedly with information sufficient to fill 3,000 encyclopedia sets.

Homo sapiens leads the genetic variety parade.

The human genome contains astounding variety potential, thanks to an estimated three billion DNA base pairs in the gene code. The original human couple carried a master mix of DNA enabling awesome variations among their descendants.

This *"random assortment of maternal and paternal sets of chromosomes at meiosis …means that each human parent carries 8,388,608 gamete possibilities…A married couple has the possibility of producing over 70 trillion different children by this process alone (8,388,608 x 8,388,608)."* [32]

There was a time when some scientists categorized human racial variances as different species, but no longer.

Today, all races are recognized as *Homo sapiens*.

Migrations to different parts of earth's geography, coupled with reliance on component portions of the pre-loaded master DNA gene pool possessed by migrating parents, guarantees descendant generation diversity.

Distinctive markers include the mother's mitochondrial DNA and the father's "Y" chromosome passed along to sons.

With more than six billion humans walking today's earth, no person's identity is lost in the shuffle. Every individual owns a one-of-a-kind set of fingerprints and a unique molecular DNA code. The 23 human chromosome pairs in the cell's nucleus contain genetic information instructing each cell how to live and to reproduce.

Fully functioning human organisms blend millions of cells, tissues and systems into a single, synchronized whole, overwhelming evolution's dogma!   For starters, the human body consists of an estimated fifty trillion cells, each composed of ten million atoms.

The tongue is the strongest body muscle. To make room for the heart, the left lung is smaller than the right.

The average human scalp has 100,000 hairs. Every square inch of the human body has an average of 32 million bacteria on it. [33]

The largest cell in the body is the female egg. The smallest is the male sperm. At the instant of conception, the human-to-be spends half an hour as a single cell.

It takes 200 muscles to take one step. Big toes have two bones each while the rest have three. A pair of human feet contain 250,000 sweat glands. About one trillion bacteria inhabit each foot.

Allegedly, the human body gives off enough heat in 30 minutes to bring half a gallon of water to a boil. The enamel in teeth is the hardest substance in the body. Teeth start developing (in gums) 6 months before birth. [34]

Humans come with a frame designed to walk upright on two legs without opposable big toes; a body needing clothing to match the weather; and language skills capable of sorting, recording and speaking thousands of words and phrases. [35]

Uniquely human reactions triggering laughter, love, compassion, and loyalty, empower pursuit of all things good. Far more than a mechanical machine, a composite human has access to the same spiritual power that guided the lives of Apostles Peter and Paul.

Humans outrank all life forms on earth other than angels.

The Bible narrative makes nearly 300 references to angels---supernatural created beings other than *Homo sapiens.*

Given dominion over all other life on earth, humans were honored to have been created in God's image, *"a little lower than the angels."* David, author of Psalms, reflects worshipful respect. *"What is man that thou art mindful of him?...Thou has made him a little lower than the angels."* [36]

The Apostle Paul confirms the existence of angels, informing they may appear among us in human form. *"Be not forgetful to entertain strangers: for thereby some have entertained angels unawares."* [37]

Ever since time zero, when *Homo sapiens* first walked the planet, striking variety shows up in individual facial appearance, hair and skin color, eye expression and body size and shape.

Racial variances distinguishing earth's inhabitants, result from migration and the isolated gene pools unique to a geographic area. Offspring of a couple representing any two isolated gene pools would only add to the diverse mix of humanity, never leading to some new and entirely different species.

"Studies have indicated the overwhelming majority of humans have a recent common ancestor within the last 5,000 years." The *"identical ancestors point …is estimated to be between 5,000 and 15,000 years ago."* [38]

Now and then overzealous headlines proclaim the début of a fossil alleged to be the common ancestor humans share with chimps or apes.

Despite strenuous spinning, huffing and puffing, persuasive evidence that any simple, single cell fossil evolved upward from some *"warm little pond"* to *Homo sapiens* status continues missing!

Humans have always existed exclusively *Sui generis*---a one-of-a-kind species!

Command Center

Human Brain

"Positive thoughts strengthen positive reaction chains

and release biochemicals, such as endorphins and serotonin,

from the brain's natural pharmacy. Bathed in these positive environments,

intellect flourishes, and with it, mental and physical health." [1]
Carolyn Leaf

© Wes Kime

Physician Wesley Kime's oil portraits are reminiscent of
John Singer Sargent's talent. Dr. Kime captured this vision
of a colleague contemplating a life-saving protocol for a patient.

Commonplace events that defy comprehension much less scientific explanation qualify as taken-for-granted "miracles."

A new human life arrives carrying the genetic characteristics of two parents, blended in a one-of-a-kind mix.

Sunbeams brighten the earth with life energizing rays powered by a super-heated furnace, all to a subdued chorus of ho-hum yawns.

And then there are those more than six billion living computers, each spinning off four billion calculations per second!

The human brain generates more electrical impulses in a single day than all the world's telephones put together.

The body package thrives with a mind loaded with creativity, capable of calculating complex equations and a freewheeling imagination able to concoct strange style theories of life's beginning.

No rational person argues an electronic personal computer designed and assembled itself by random reactions of inert matter. Paradoxically, some intelligent minds insist human brains originated accidentally from a non-intelligent source, without design or designer!

Intelligent reasoning power from unintelligent matter?

Where's the logic? Where's the evidence?

Talk about a leap of "faith!"

If human brains can concoct theories suggesting life evolved from non-life, why can't man's intelligence create that first ever, living cell that supposedly created itself accidentally?

Gene expression profiles, residing in the brain's cerebral cortex, differ significantly between chimps and humans. Comparing the two, *"…it seems that the brain is really special in that humans have accelerated patterns of gene activity."* [2]

Give credit where credit is due.

No reputable university has awarded a Ph.D. to a chimp.

Cute pets display clever behavior but never come close to an academic level warranting a kindergarten graduation certificate.

Chimps and dogs understand many human language words. Parrots and Lyrebirds mimic sounds and many spoken words and phrases.

The fact remains: no animal brain matches the mind of *Homo sapiens.*

The human brain works creative wonders, thanks to a built-in pump and circulatory system. The heart and the brain function jointly as mutually dependent colleagues. Without a constant flow of blood to the brain, death arrives momentarily.

Brains orchestrate action in mega dimension beyond the capability of the most intricately designed electronic computer. A single brain cell is said to be able to hold five times as much information as contained in a set of printed Encyclopedia Britannica.

England's Stephen Wiltshire, a twenty-first century phenomenon, owns a brain that staggers imaginations of other mortals.

Give Wiltshire a quick helicopter tour around London or Rome, and within a few short days he can draw what he saw on a curving, wall-sized stretch of paper. Doors, windows, roof designs, in right numbers and locations---an entire cityscape, all from memory.

Reasoning capability develops from a genetic code in place at conception, nine-months before birth.

Thanks to DNA inherited from two parents, all creative thought, sensory reaction, speech, and memory are driven by *"a three-pound brain…composed of twelve billion neurons…with…120 trillion connections"* encased in a trauma-resistant, compact, cranial container. [3]

That memory bank *"consists of about ten thousand million nerve cells.*

"Each nerve cell puts out somewhere in the region of between ten thousand and one hundred thousand connecting fibres [fibers] by which it makes contact with other nerve cells in the brain. Altogether, the total number of connections in the human brain approaches 10^{15} or a thousand-million-million…

"Imagine an area about half the size of the USA (one million square miles) covered in a forest of trees containing ten thousand trees per square mile. If each tree contained one hundred thousand leaves the total number of leaves in the forest would be 10^{15}, equivalent to the number of connections in the human brain!" [4]

© Nadezhda V. Kulagina

**In thinking mode, the human brain's one-billion
neurons perform an estimated 4 billion transactions per second.**

Consider the challenge confronting the world's most skilled electrician attempting to mastermind the wiring of that jungle of copper requiring a thousand-million-million connections without miswiring, short-circuiting, or blowing a fuse!

If that doesn't deflate the ignorance of egocentric arrogance, try confining that jumble to the micro dimensions of a three-pound brain fitted snugly within the custom-designed, bony cranium that offers something less than 100 cubic inches of spatial capacity!

So this feat of electrical/biological engineering supposedly designed and installed its own wiring diagram mechanism without so much as a master plan or Designer?

Humans, endowed with this incomparable "computer," are supposed to believe it evolved over many millions-of-years thanks to billions of trial-and-error, undirected, mindless, random mutations?

Without blown fuses?

Hong Kong neurosurgeon C. P. Yu sees the human brain as *"the most complex 3 pound structure of this Universe."*

A Fellow of the Hong Kong College of Surgeons, Dr. Yu describes the *"basic unit"* consisting *"of a neurone and glial cells"* with at least *"10 to 30 billion neurons and ten times that number of glial cells.*

"Each neurone has 10,000 to 50,000 interconnections with other neurones. Electron microscopy differentiates excitatory from inhibitory neurones by the presence of a micro-spine." [5]

The nucleus of each neuron contains a *"DNA molecule"* which if unraveled would stretch a meter in length *"within a cell 1/30,000 the size of a pinhead."* [5]

Eight layers of bone with a *"thick irregular plate"* at the base *"with openings for cranial nerves, blood vessels, and the spinal cord"* compose a geometrically designed skull encasing the brain. Inside the skull, *"the brain is surrounded by pressurized cerebrospinal fluid…providing nutrition and providing an active suspension system for the brain."* [5]

Smooth movement of a coordinated body is taken for granted---until upset by the insidious Parkinson's disease which disrupts basal ganglia function.

"…A tiny structure called the Subthalamic Nucleus (STN) is the pacemaker of the body. Numerous feedback loops and connections between the STN and other nuclei within the entire basal ganglia are responsible for the ultra-smoothness of movements." [5]

The brain orders the hand to automatically jerk away instantly from a too hot surface without conscious thought. The skin's power of touch equips the brain to respond to the hint of pain or to velvet's gentle caress.

Dr. Yu reminds that this message center for human life, manages five senses: smell, taste, hearing, touch, and vision. Feel, taste, sound, and smell impact thought processes that activate the full range of human emotions.

The brain *"can distinguish more than 10,000 odors through tiny olfactory nerves at the roof of our nose."* [5] And with that delicate sense of smell operational, taste buds introduce discriminating gourmets to the joys of dining.

Thanks to two ears with stereo capability, humans listen to and identify the direction of multi-directional sound. Three miniature bones, tiniest in the body, anchor the listening process.

Each ear comes equipped with *"24,000 'hair cells', which convert vibrations to electrical impulses."* The hearing nerve *"enters the internal auditory meatus which houses 3 other nerves, 2 vestibular and 1 facial nerve, all tightly packed together and yet never pose any electrical leak or cross-over distortion."* [5]

The human eye completes this complex array of power!

According to Dr. Yu, *"Apart from having auto-focus, auto-exposure, excellent low light response, excellent depth perception that no camera comes close, the eye can perceive: 1. Velocity, 2. Direction, 3. Location, 4. Texture, 5. Identity, and 6. Color."* [5]

The neurosurgeon's summation exposes the preposterous notion of evolution's discordant dilemma, which attempts to account for the human brain's genesis. Screened through mathematical analysis of probability, complexity of this magnitude surpasses impossible.

"What is the probability of life arising from atoms to molecules, amino acids to protein (don't forget all life proteins are left-handed in configuration), DNA to messenger RNA, single cell to sexual reproduction, all the way to the human body with wonders of the brain and its senses, the heart and the circulation, the clotting cascade, the immune system, the wound repair and healing mechanisms?

"Bear in mind that all these have to go against the second law of thermodynamics, [the] law of irreducible complexity, and the fact that most mutations are harmful." [5]

The average human heart does its thing---beating rhythmically 100,800 times a day (with a pulse rate of 70 beats per minute) while pumping ten tons of blood daily, the weight equivalent of 140 adult humans. [6]

And here the plot thickens!

Already loaded with enough DNA in one microscopic cell to stretch from the earth to the moon and to dictate physical design, the brain is poised to absorb and record information from every sight, sound, smell and touch encountered in a lifetime.

This acquired information is the raw material feeding the thought process that triggers responsive action. Anyone reacting to the flash of pain from touching a hot stove doesn't need the vote of a committee to instruct the hurting hand to move from the danger.

Reaction time boggles minds---some say the brain processes data as fast as four billion transactions per second!

Thoughts produce action. When all is in sync, it doesn't take a genius to remove a hurting hand instantly from a hot stove.

There is danger that the cacophony of competing sounds and the blizzard of visual data confronting twenty-first century human brains can overwhelm its capacity to reason wisely. Despite the brain's remarkable information processing capability, anything more than seven items can compromise the brain's working memory.

"People faced with a plethora of choices are apt to make no decision at all…

" 'A decision is harder if the amount of information you have to juggle is greater.' The proliferation of choices can create paralysis when the stakes are high and the information complex." [7]

All thoughts, whether good or evil, trigger attitudes and emotions. The composite thought process shapes character.

An individual's ability to discover and accept the truth about God can be lost in the crescendo of information overload that attacks the senses.

"As he [a person] *thinketh in his heart, so is he."* [8]

"Positive attitudes cause the secretion of the correct amount of chemicals, and negative attitudes distort the chemical secretions in a way that disrupts their natural flow.

"The chemicals are like little cellular signals that translate the information of your thoughts into a physical reality in your body and mind, creating an emotion. The combination of thoughts, emotions and resulting attitudes, impacts your body in a positive or negative way." [9]

Patterns of toxic thoughts tend to put human immune systems at risk!

Buried feelings of anger, fear, anxiety and bitterness create volcanic buildups in your body. When you internalize wounded emotions, you allow a seething mix of anger, hostility and resentment to develop." [10]

A life drowning in evil thoughts, not only can resort to hate crimes and senseless murders, but also imposes a death sentence on the thinker as a long-term consequence.

"Forgiveness is a choice…there is increasing scientific evidence that forgiveness gives us healthier and happier lives…

"When people hold onto their anger and past trauma, the stress response stays active, making them sick mentally and physically." [11]

© Yellow

**Recognizing the brain as the body's "situation room,"
confirms beauty is much more than skin deep.**

Injustice, assassinations and wars result when personal anger, bitterness and hate is projected into a community, with ripple consequences infecting nations and governments.

Without forgiveness, festering hatreds spawn war with its death curse.

Peace begins with forgiveness---and a smile!

Hatred generates stress, corroding the soul. In contrast, a personal, living faith inspires forgiveness, extending even to enemies who despitefully use and abuse.

It may not sound like a joy ride to return good for evil and to forgive no less than *"seventy time seven,"* but when it does happen, it demonstrates the power to forgive comes directly from the Creator of light and life.

While dying in excruciating pain, Christ forgave his tormentors with the words, *"Father forgiver them for they know not what they do."* [12]

God forgives all sins and any sinner who asks forgiveness. [13] The truly forgiven follow Christ's example---the exclusive route to inner, personal peace.

The same Scripture that describes the miraculous origin of first life also offers the formula for abundant living.

"Get rid of all bitterness, rage and anger, brawling and slander, along with every form of malice. Be kind and compassionate to one another, forgiving each other, must as in Christ, God forgave you." [14]

The Creator pointed listeners to the merits of positive thinking that leads to the good life, assuring all mankind, *"I have come that they may have life, and have it to the full."* [15]

Good-bye "True Science," Hello *"Phantasy [sic]."*

Charles Darwin's conjecture, built on a series of unproven assumptions, runs counter to natural law's predictability.

True science resonates precision and predictability!

Toss a ball into the air and the law of gravity kicks in. The Periodic Table of the Elements provides a consistently reliable base for building chemical formulas. Ecological balance assures a life-friendly environment. Mendel's law of inheritance offers verifiable genetic results.

Its been said, *"Nature is the Book of God."*

Surrounded by the bounties of a balanced biosystem, its logical to sense the presence and creative power of a *"Superior Rationality."*

Evolution's raw rejection of design put in place by a Master Designer, reinterprets nature as merely a *"Book of Random Accident,"* side-stepping confirmation of God's miraculous touch in the creation of life on earth.

The upside-down paradox rings scientifically sinister!

Easily recognizable, pervasive evidence pointing to God's creative power has been twisted and overridden in an effort to convince gullible minds that life created itself accidentally in a *"warm little pond"* at some unknown time and place, millions of years before the present!

Evolution responds with deafening silence when challenged to explain just how human intelligence, centered in the human brain, managed to manufacture itself and to acquire information from a non-living, unintelligent source.

Fence-straddling theists, swallowing evolution's bait, discount the authority of Scripture and the supremacy of the Lord God Almighty, while clinging feebly to superficial "faith" in a diminished, unrecognizable god.

Darwin's tortured trail of flawed genealogy pushes mankind off the lofty pedestal of presiding leadership at earth's command center. Humans are downgraded to just another *"biologic transit stop"* moving aimlessly on a treadmill to oblivion.

Darwin fretted his grandiose scheme seemed *"…a mere rag of an hypothesis with as many flaw[s] & holes as sound parts."* [16]

True science has yet to corroborate his wishful thinking. In fact, the *"holes"* have widened to chasms and the *"flaws"* exposed as empty bubbles of irrelevancy.

In legal parlance, a cascade of exceptions "eats up the rule." Evolution's roster of *"flaws"* and *"holes"* devour any semblance of a rule that may have been used to bolster and propagate a tarnished icon.

One-hundred-fifty years after *Origin's* November 24, 1859 début, and counting, scientific knowledge has exploded but has been less than kind to a bankrupt concept, drowning in suspicious rhetoric.

The very definition of science, bent grotesquely out-of-shape by evolution's montage of assumptions, abstractions and suppositions, ends in a cul-de-sac of gross error. Evolution theory, in a variety of formats, has infiltrated human thinking insidiously for several thousand years. Heavy doses of hype and bias, have kept it in play.

Lacking rhyme, reason or respectability, the hypothesis manages to survive in the minds of imaginative humans, too proud to acknowledge the presence and oversight of a Higher Power, the Author of all science.

With a faint whiff of prescience, Charles Robert Darwin himself confessed doubts about his grand scheme, worrying that he may *"have devoted my life to a phantasy."* [17]

He had cause to worry!

Darwin's *"phantasy"* mirrored dreams of empire that rejected recognition of the Creator and categorised some human beings as subservient to others. In contrast, 56 stouthearted guys in Philadelphia had earlier turned their back on fantasy, staking their lives, fortunes and sacred honor on the premise that *"all men are created equal."*

Commitment to *"unalienable rights"* bestowed by God, the *"Creator"* of all life, anchored the legal framework for the birth of a nation. The operative words, *"equal"* and *"created,"* echoed each time the liberty bell chimed.

Darwin's evolution fiction never was, isn't now, and never will be!

"The God who made the world and everything in it is the Lord of heaven and earth…He himself gives all men life and breath and everything else…From one man he made every nation of men, that they should inhabit the whole earth…" [18]

IX

Six Billion Plus Miracles

It's About Us

"I find as difficult to understand a scientist who does not
acknowledge the existence of a superior rationality
behind the existence of the universe as it is to comprehend
a theologian who would deny the advance of science." [1]

Wernher von Braun

© Warren L. Johns

All human cultures share the *Homo sapiens* genetic code.
Every person, like these bright eyed Hong Kong youngsters,
carries a one-of-a-kind genetic fingerprint

Its not everyday an unmarked envelope, loaded with $1200 cash, is lost on a public street in front of a fast-food restaurant, waiting for some curious pedestrian to discover.

But that's exactly what happened in downtown Murfreesboro, Tennessee, one March day in 2010. The event made headlines because once found, the unusual circumstances surrounding the discovery guaranteed widespread interest.

More than a year into the deepest economic downturn since the "Great Depression" early in the twenty-first century, and with unemployment reaching double digits, this kind of "mini-fortune" never grows on trees--- and rarely on city sidewalks.

Typically, the finder might have pocketed the loose cash, reasoning "finders keepers, losers etc…" Fortunately for the owner/loser, the sharp-eyed young guy who spotted the windfall, proved to be anything but typical!

Rather than depositing to his personal bank account, he entrusted the stash to the police in quest of the legitimate owner.

That's the upside of the story.

The downside soon followed as a surprising number of dishonest, greedy citizens reached out, pushing fictitious "claims" to steal the loot.

When put to the test, the cheaters couldn't properly describe the envelope, the number and denominations of the bills much less the location in the city where the loss occurred.

As the old saying goes, "truth will out" and justice stepped in.

The lucky owner, a truck driver, had no problem identifying his loss. Even before the police returned the $1200 to him, he met the good Samaritan finder and said "thank-you" with a $100 reward.

Goodness lives and thrives, even in the midst of a world overrun with the contagious virus of rampaging evil.

An old Cherokee told his grandson about a battle that goes on inside people. He said, "My son, the battle is between two wolves inside us all.

"One is Evil - It is anger, envy, jealousy, sorrow, regret, greed, arrogance, self-pity, guilt, resentment, inferiority, lies, false pride, superiority, and ego.

"The other is Good - It is joy, peace, love, hope, serenity, humility, kindness, benevolence, empathy, generosity, truth, compassion and faith."

The grandson thought about it for a minute and then asked his grandfather: "Which wolf wins?"

The old Cherokee simply replied, "The one you feed."

Internet, Ando---World of Color

Legend's Diogenes traversed the world, carrying a lighted lantern, looking for an honest man. If he had lived in the computer age, he could have found him, right there in Murfreesboro, Tennessee.

Good and evil compete to control human minds and hearts---typically conflicting within the same person.

Evolution theory offers no litmus test distinguishing right from wrong. *Malum en se* (wrong in itself), shifts and drifts, defined by the lowest common denominator in a prevalent culture. In a 1998 Darwin Day keynote address, one Darwinist admitted as much.

"No gods worth having exist; No life after death exists; No ultimate foundation for ethics exists; No ultimate meaning in life exists; Human free will is nonexistent." [2]

Evolution's dark philosophy---beginning in some *"warm little pond"* and ending in certain death---is a slave to darkness. Evolution points only to indiscriminate darkness where *"no ultimate foundation for ethics exists."*

To extrapolate from the real to authenticate evolution's never-was, spreads an intellectual virus, infecting minds with toxic fraud. Preachers of this pernicious, secular religion, seduce converts by calling the shots in a dark dance to nowhere.

Beyond philosophical speculation, evolution spawns a myth exposing humans to cultural darkness. With nothing but survival of the fittest in play, what evolves is anything but a pretty picture!

A furious Cain, in a fit of jealous rage, murdered his brother Abel.

Before committing suicide, Adolph Hitler's blood lust snuffed out millions of lives with abandon. Twenty-first century merchants of hate, misrepresenting themselves as God's agents, exemplify criminal cowardice; indiscriminately killing human beings they've never met.

Life's Creator epitomizes light! The Genesis account of the miracle of life's origins opens doors to ten rules for enhanced living and defines the sharp difference between good and evil.

When human ego succumbs to pride's seductive intoxication and evil infects the soul, the golden rule is tarnished, overwhelmed by an unconscionable greed that tramples property rights, degrading life.

Unselfish caregivers, concerned for the health and well being of others while exhibiting low levels of aggression, tend to find peace of mind and longer life expectancies. [3]

There is reason to believe bully behavior delivers stress levels attacking the immune system while inducing an array of destructive heart and circulatory symptoms leading to disease.

Intolerance is symptomatic of insecurity. Evolution's intolerance of the truth about God and His creation exposes a failed culture.

Peace begins with a smile---and a clear conscience.

It's an irrational paradox to assert human intelligence derives its reasoning power from some unknown, unintelligent source!

Human brain power from inert matter? An inanimate rock?

To assert human creative capacity originated from a non-creative, inferior, inanimate source ignores *"rationality."* When it comes to power to hang the moon, mere mortal genius lacks the *"superior rationality"* envisioned by rocket scientist Wernher von Braun as the ultimate power *"behind the existence of the universe."* [4] The power source for gravity, magnetism, electricity and human thought derives from that *"superior rationality."*

Despite contrary myth, true science and true religion are not mutually exclusive. The two disciplines flourish compatibly. Reasoning that examines and evaluates all evidence objectively, anchors and inspires both science and religion. Rational faith binds science and religion in an inextricably commingled package.

True religion is more than theological theory and high-flying rhetoric, floating abstractly in clouds. Belief in the Creator of life is central to the understanding of life's origin, purpose, goal and ultimate destination.

Science is fact! The Creator of the universe is its Author!

True science bows to its Author.

Six billion plus human miracles walk the face of Planet Earth, each person invested with the mental skill to discover and design, the power to reason, and to discriminate right from wrong.

Taken for granted, the birth of a baby is an every-day miracle!

Created in God's image, humans are more than an elaborate composite of rare physical prowess guided by minds capable of orchestrating music and launching rockets to the moon. The cohesive whole reaches out for a spiritual power that unleashes boundless dimensions of reason, communication and creativity.

Apes, chimps and monkeys don't sing songs, *Homo sapiens* do.

Human physical presence, powered by the mind's genius, has achieved astounding feats of creativity since ancient times. People write books, travel in space; produce movies; play golf; compose melodies; design instruments; orchestrate symphonies; build bridges and monuments; and invent machines as complex as a computer and as simple as a mousetrap.

Works of art from the hearts and souls of Rembrandt, John Singer Sargent and Winslow Homer didn't appear on canvass as a result of a chimp swishing a brush dipped in a rainbow of oils.

The likes of Leonardo DaVinci, Albert Einstein, and Galileo Galilei were born with mental acuity capable of sorting out heavy doses of information powering rare levels of creative genius. The phenomenal human brain possesses capacity for prodigious memory feats!

Whether myth or hyperbole, tradition reports Pliny the Elder, a Roman scholar, authored *Natural History*, a literary work suggesting Cyrus the Great, the Achaemenian King of Persia, *"knew the names of all the men in his army."* Allegedly, Lucius Scipio was familiar with *"the names of all the people of Rome"* and *"Mithridates of Pontus knew the languages of all the twenty-two peoples in his domains."* [5]

Thomas Cranmer, Archbishop of Canterbury, is reputed to have memorized the entire Bible in three months. A blindfolded chess-master, George Koltanowski, played 56 matches simultaneously in a nine-hour marathon, winning fifty games while tying the other six. [5]

Then there's the occasional genius that astounds other high IQ elites.

Consider Wolfgang Amadeus Mozart who walked the earth for a brief 35-years, composing volumes of musical scores that continue to enchant concert aficionados.

A six-year-old Mozart made his first public virtuoso appearance in Linz. At ten, he performed a symphony of his own in Amsterdam.

In April, 1770, Amadeus visited Rome's Sistine Chapel where he listened to Allegri's *Miserere.* The Vatican reserved the complex musical for private concerts presented to honored guests. The 14-year-old genius listened intently and later accessed his masterful memory to reproduce the entire score in flawless detail.

"Since we are surrounded by such a great cloud of witnesses...
Let us run with perseverance the race marked out for us...
and fix our eyes on Jesus, the author and perfecter of our faith." [6]

"A great cloud of witnesses," committed to *"the Way,"* demonstrate the power of good trumping evil.

Saul of Tarsus, a Roman citizen born of Hebrew parents, patrolled first century streets determined to root out the rapidly spreading Christian "heresy." In Saul's mind, half-measures wouldn't do. In an all-or-nothing context, the issue in his mind loomed right or wrong, life or death.

Belligerent intolerance gave no quarter. Once discovered by Saul's henchmen, any Christian faced a potential death sentence. Saul launched his anti-Christian hate crusade after standing-by, a witness to the stoning of Steven who met his fate, devoting his life to the *"Righteous One."*

Saul had seen Steven fall to his knees and heard him cry, " '*Lord do not hold this sin against them.' When he had said this, he fell asleep."* [7]

Tasting blood, Saul went on a rampage, intent on destroying the fledgling church. *"Going from house to house, he dragged off men and women and put them in prison."* [8]

Zealous to a fault, Saul took his self-appointed task seriously, *"breathing out murderous threats against the Lord's disciples."* [9] He obtained letters of introduction to synagogues in Damascus, intending to find *"any there who belonged to the Way, whether men or women,"* [9] determined to take them prisoner to Jerusalem, intending to do all he could to crush the Christian faith.

En route to Damascus, his mission did an abrupt about face! A blinding light sent him sprawling to the ground, and an unseen voice instructed him to continue to Damascus where he would be told what to do.

The Creator of life on earth appeared personally to this brilliant man of honest conviction, both redirecting his mission and transforming his heart.

In a flash, Saul, the persecutor, became Paul, the persecuted.

Born to Hebrew parents, the gutsy apostle possessed the privilege of Roman citizenship with ready access to its empire. He put these credentials to work in pursuit of his new mission. He sailed the Mediterranean three times, sharing the good news and founding Christian congregations. His time, talent and resources were devoted exlusively to all things good.

Paul the Apostle supported himself by making tents; he faced hostile audiences without fear; he presented the truth about God to political leaders; sometimes he ran for his life, narrowly escaping death; other times he went to prison for his bold presentations.

Ultimately he suffered a martyr's death, beheaded in Rome.

Paul taught the Genesis account of creation, warning first century Christians *"the man of lawlessness…opposes and exalts himself over everything that is called God or is worshiped, and even set himself up…proclaiming himself to be God."* [10]

Other than willingly giving his life, Paul's legacy of letters provided key components of the New Testament that preserved a clear picture of God's truth with its promise of life eternal, the reward of all people committed to the power and saving grace of Christ the Creator.

During the two thousand years since Paul's journey to Damascus was rerouted, a vast multitude of devout men and women have joined the international fellowship of believers, living lives of faith in action.

During World War II's raging fury, when sixty million human lives were snuffed out, Christian men and women stood tall, in the tradition of the Apostle Paul, risking their own lives to save others!

Heroes like South Sea Islander chief Kato Ragoso, Cpl. Desmond Doss, and John Weidner put it all on the line for humanity's greater good.

Kato Ragoso, raised in a culture accustomed to vengeance killing, rejected a pagan heritage, embraced Christianity and dedicated his considerable talents to telling the world the truth about God.

Photo courtesy of Dr. Don Moran

Kato Ragoso, courageous Christian leader, risked his life to rescue sailors and airmen from Pacific Ocean waters while WW II raged. He is pictured here during a 1936 California visit.

Visitors to a 1936 church convention in San Francisco, were treated to the gentle voice and dignified demeanor of this Christian gentleman, a mere generation removed from a culture of violence.

Facing death each day, Kato organized his countrymen in life-saving missions. Without pay or fame, his team of unsung heroes, patrolled Pacific waters, using a fleet of locally crafted canoes to rescue hundreds of struggling military men from capture or drowning.

Future U.S. President, John F. Kennedy, was saved by Ragoso's team!

By strange irony, this brilliant and courageous Solomon Island leader who inspired hundreds of life-saving acts, would possibly have been viewed a *"savage"* if measured by Darwin's blind racism.

It wasn't Western Europe's elite culture that miraculously transformed Ragoso's life into righteousness, but the Christian faith that powered his soul.

When Desmond T. Doss, a humble Christian from the American south, served the United States Army as an unarmed medic during World War II, he took his faith with him, kneeling to pray bunk-side in Army barracks, before retiring, despite taunts.

Internet – My Hero

World War II medic, Cpl. Desmond T. Doss, was awarded the Congressional Medal of Honor for selfless courage.

All bullying derision disappeared once the 77th division launched into the Battle of Okinawa and encountered *"a heavy concentration of artillery, mortar and machinegun fire"* on *"Hacksaw Ridge."*

The only medic available to a 155-man company, the twice-wounded Doss, displayed *"courage above and beyond the call of duty" by* repeatedly exposing himself to the withering barrage sweeping the Maeda Escarpment and single-handedly rescuing more than 70 wounded soldiers.

John Henry Weidner, devout Christian, born in France of Dutch parents, risked his life aiding more than 1,000 men and women to avoid capture by the Nazis. The famed "Dutch-Paris" underground was organized and fearlessly led by John and his sister, Gabrielle.

John, a master of disguise, was arrested by enemy occupiers more than once but always managed to outwit his captors and to escape.

As for Gabrielle, the Nazis stormed a Paris church in the midst of a worship service, and unceremoniously whisked her away to a concentration camp. She didn't survive the horrors of camp life.

Wikepedia

More than 1,000 men and women avoided capture by the Nazis during World War II, thanks to the "Dutch-Paris" underground organized by John Henry Weidner and his sister, Gabrielle.

After World War II's blood bath ended, France, Great Britain, Holland and the United States honored John's selfless courage by awarding medals of distinction.

The most persuasive sermons are lived, not preached from a pulpit.

More than mechanically articulating the truth about God, true believers invite the power that created the universe by *"the word of the Lord,"* to enter the heart and to guide the life, embracing the same power source that created life and hung the moon.

Recognition of the reality of the creation miracle doesn't make you a Christian anymore than stepping into a garage makes you a car. Church pews house those who walk the walk side-by-side with the mean spirited who profess a *"form of godliness."*

Individuals adopt a personal value system ranging from aspirations for all things good to the depths of dark evil. Self-centered takers hurt and destroy what they touch,, spreading doom and gloom. Others return good for evil reflecting the example of their Creator and the ten rules for more abundant, happier living outlined in Exodus 20.

Reverent recognition of the Creator as the exclusive source of life is one thing! Realization that humans have been created to reflect God's image and to connect to this power source humbles the honest hearted.

The roster of unsung Christian heroes represents a vast multitude!

Insurance exec, "Stubby" Wall; clergyman Art Patzer; patient school teacher, Helen Johnson; community leader, Clyde Unglesbee; and three memorable Michigan gentlemen surnamed Salisbury, Travis and Wheaton.

Others crossing my path include Singapore's Peter Foo; Russia's Michael Kulukov; Spain's Daniel Basterra Montserrat; creation's champion, Henry M. Morris; and Charlene Morrison Johns, the mother who gave me life.

These, gentle Christians, many who have gone to their rest, have, by faith, reached out to the Lord God Almighty for guidance and the spiritual power to walk in His footsteps. Any person, walking with God, constitutes a majority, overwhelming darkness with the light of eternal life.

"It takes just one solitary light to guide a thousand ships in from the night." [11]

X

Life Conquers Death

Original, Unborrowed, Underrived

"King of Kings. Lord of Lords.
He shall reign forever and ever." [1]

George Frederic Handel

© egd

An artist's perception of "Christ the Redeemer," crowns
Rio de Janeiro's Corcovado. The outstretched arms invite
all people to accept the "Good News" from the cross.
"I am the way, the truth, and the life." [2]

"It is finished" were the last words heard from the anguished lips of a victim suffering excruciating pain, condemned to a death of cruel and unusual punishment by a tyrannical regime that had contempt for human life and equated justice with the power of the sword.

That Friday afternoon, early in the first century A.D., changed earth history forever and played to a larger audience in the cosmic theater of the universe.

Face bleeding from a crown of thorns jammed onto his head; taunted with a purple robe mocking kingly power; struck in the face; Christ endured a public flogging---all before being found guilty of anything.

His crime: three years serving a suppressed populace with a message of healing, hope, and happiness. After questioning Jesus of Nazareth, the pathetic Pilate declared, *"I find no basis for a charge against Him."* [3]

Still, the unruly mob ruled the courtyard chaos!

In a dark-of-night trial, an innocent thirty-three-year-old was sent to His death by Pilate, a weak-kneed political hack, intimidated by frenzied fanatics that thumbed collective noses at legal due process.

Christ surrendered His life on the Cross, voluntarily!

 Execution by death on a cross represented Roman "justice" at its worst. A jeering crowd trailed His steps as Roman soldiers placed a cross on His shoulders and led the way to Jerusalem's *hill of a skull*, the execution site.

© MaxFX

Torture was added to the mix by nailing the hands and feet to rough, tree-cut lumber, and then thrusting the upright device into the ground to maximize hurt. Left to writhe in pain for hours, or even days, until the victim took a final gasp of breath.

Cruel and unusual punishment even for the most despicable criminal.

In this case, the apparent triumph of evil, changed world history. Christ the Creator, God's son in human form, lived and died to demonstrate to the universe that Lucifer's hatred, would kill even God, if he could.

The Scriptural lexicon defines evil as sin.

Lucifer the "light bearer," a high ranking created being, overcome by pride and jealousy, challenged God's authority, justice, and love, and stirred doubts, resentment and rebellion in the hearts of other angels.

Sin deceives the *"very elect,"* delivering death.

Had God suppressed the rebellion by destroying Satan, the act would appear to justify the charge of tyranny with the result that other created beings, fearful for their own lives, would be inclined to serve God from fear rather than free choice inspired by love.

Instead, the adversary of all things good was cast from God's heavenly presence and confined to earth, center stage for a raging spiritual battle demonstrating the tragic consequences of evil destined to be witnessed by a universal audience.

The Genesis narrative describes the cunning deception of Satan, the fallen Lucifer, now God's adversary determined to mar a perfect creation and to recruit humans to join his rebellion.

Sin's ripple effect disfigures perfection and devours life---casualties of the spiritual war pitting good versus evil.

Despite imposition of death's curse imposed on mankind for disobedience and failure to trust, God offered a *"way of escape"* through the plan of redemption demonstrating His love and fairness.

Inescapably, the plan imposed death as sin's wage.

God's son paid that cost for all sinners. Had God the Father died to demonstrate His love for humans, Satan would have won. So God sent His *"only begotten son,"* whose life and ministry demonstrated ultimate love.

Christ's death on the cross, revealed Satan's hatred and God's unbounded love and commitment to all humans choosing to believe. God's Spirit, with His power for forgiveness and love, justifies the life of any human choosing to believe.

Until Christ visited earth in person, the image of original power and created perfection blurred, lost in trivia and a cosmic jumble. Jesus, of

Nazareth, the greatest life ever lived on Planet Earth, arrived with less than auspicious human credentials.

He was born in a barn, burdened by rumors of suspect parentage.

Surrounded by poverty, Jesus lived in a culture gasping for survival under the brutal heel of Rome's ruthless "iron empire."

Robust, bronzed and brawny, He served an apprenticeship in Joseph's carpenter shop. Less than a bed-of-roses environment, corruption shrouded the streets and alleys of his home village.

Aware of the town's notoriety, cynics raised eyebrows, asking rhetorically, *"Can any good thing come out of Nazareth?"*

© Nathan Greene

Christ never had a bank account, owned a home, wrote a book, held political office, or commanded a military force.

Exuding charismatic personal charm, all it took were the words, "follow me" for twelve young men to join his unique ministry of hope, goodness and the promise of abundant living today and a forever life to come.

His disciples followed with no promise of pay or explanation of just where He would lead. No one asked about perks. They accepted his invitation in faith---simply because he said, *"Come, follow me and I will make you fishers of men."*

Some misunderstood the invite, hoping the Messiah would deliver subjugated citizens from the political heel of the Roman oppressor.

Despite lack of academic credentials, He taught thousands, captivating minds with a message of love, forgiveness, and a formula for peace. No microphone boosted the sound of His words.

He lived and led by example from the geographic crossroads of world commerce. Without access to mass media, news of His words and deeds traveled with lightning speed. No media blitz publicized his appearances. Rumors that Jesus worked miracles, focused attention to His ministry.

He didn't sermonize from the altar of a cathedral or a pulpit in an arena seating thousands.

Still, thousands followed His footsteps, captivated by a message that echoed across cultures and two millenniums into the future.

When a wedding celebration ran out of wine, He transformed water into prime vintage by His word alone. Powered by His blessing, five loaves of bread and two fish satisfied the hunger of a crowd of 5,000.

With the curse of incurable leprosy running rampant, hearts beat faster and eyebrows raised with news He restored vibrant health to ten lepers.

Responding to His command, an infirm man *"took up his bed and walked."* Restoring sight to a blind man startled observers who witnessed the incredible scene.

The countryside pondered His wisdom and responded to His leadership. Looking for clues to empowerment, hundreds followed Him to a natural, outdoor setting on the slope of a hillside. Tickets were not required.

He spoke with authority.

But to the surprise and chagrin of some who came prepared to take up arms against the Roman occupier, He offered words to inspire the human spirit instead, blazing a trail to inner peace and future promise.

He predicted the *"meek"* would *"inherit the earth."*

"Blessed are the merciful, for they shall be shown mercy. Blessed are the peacemakers, for they shall be called the children of God...." [4]

Contrary to epic notions of heroic history built around military conquest with its harvest of death and destruction, Christ created original life and preached peace and the sanctity of life.

He urged listeners to seek right; to be pure in heart; to love enemies; to forgive up to seven-times-seventy; and to reconcile with adversaries. As the antithesis of darkness, he reminded followers:

"You are the light of the world…Let your light shine before men that they may see your good deeds and praise your Father in heaven." [5]

The words sounded a call to spiritual arms, not military action!

This formula for a better life opened the door to personal peace and abundant living. It came with the gift of a Divine Comforter, empowering believers to transform to a new and improved version of themselves.

Although Christ committed no crime, His human body died the death of a criminal, an innocent victim of man's inhumanity to man.

Within minutes after His death, He was buried in haste. No funeral or memorial service honored His life. Nor was He recognized with public burial rites featuring eloquent rhetoric.

Joseph of Arimathaea volunteered his own family's tomb, chiseled from hillside rock, as a final resting place. But the "rest" was not to be "final."

After the Sabbath, early the first day of the week, the seal of the tomb was broken, the stone entry door rolled away, and Christ rose, forever victorious over death.

The crucifixion events crowned by the resurrection miracle, described in the writings of Mathew, Mark, Luke and John, are preserved for all to read in the Biblical cannon composed of Old and New Testaments compiled by devout Christian leaders late in the fourth century A.D.

Christ's immaculately conceived birth, flawless life in the midst of an evil environment, cruel crucifixion and unselfish death, crowned by the resurrection miracle, is unmatched in other belief systems.

Ironically, some of the same evolutionists who doubt Christ's resurrection, somehow manage to believe life on earth created itself from non-living matter, accidentally, by spontaneous generation.

Christ, the Creator and source of all life on earth, exemplified God's absolute justice and patient love for humanity, demonstrating unlimited Divine power---not just to hang the sun and the moon but also to conquer death's curse.

The Scriptural "Big Picture" narrative, written over a 1500 year time span, begins with Moses' Genesis account of the creation miracle and concludes with John's Revelation describing Christ's return to earth bringing life eternal to all who believe.

Christ's ministry revolutionized history!

Christ's unassailable victory over death, as reported and recorded by living witnesses, left God's adversary no option but to surrender to failure or to attempt to rewrite history by launching a frontal attack.

Having deceived Adam and Eve in the Garden of Eden, the diabolical prevaricator initiated the same deceptive strategy to discredit God by depicting the Scriptural narrative as myth and life on earth as nothing more than a mindless, evolving accident.

Conjecturing that life originated millions of years in the ancient past in some unidentified *"warm little pond"* echoes the fiction. Some of earth's brightest minds swallow the insidious line!

Life on earth didn't start accidentally by spontaneous generation in some rocky, *"warm little pond!"* The miracle of life is a gift from the Rock of Ages.

The Truth About God

It's About Him

"You are not an accident…You were made by God and for God, and until you understand that, life will never make sense. Only in God do we discover our origin, our identity, our meaning, our purpose, our significance, and our destiny." [1]

Rick Warren

© Alan Collins, sculptor, Loma Linda University Medical Center

A sobering look at distorted mischaracterizations of the Creator plaguing the culture of Charles Darwin's era, may help explain his cynical take in his quest for a secular explanation for life's origin.

Darwin must have smiled with pride at thought of Annie, his ten-year-old daughter. Understandably, he would have been virtually inconsolable when he lost her to death in 1851, squeezing joy from his life.

Europe's conflicted religious history offered meager solace to a father's aching heart. The influential naturalist likely witnessed pro-forma caretakers of faith *"having a form of godliness but denying its power,"* [2] misrepresenting the Creator.

Eight years after Annie's death, *The Origin of Species* was published with its dark, jaundiced view, depicting life as meaningless, luck-of-the-draw.

Deceitful evil disguised as "good" misrepresents God.

Institutionalized religion, when subsidized and imposed on the public by the state's secular power, can propagate meaningless rhetoric diminishing and distorting the truth about God. Fraudulent caricature defames God as vindictive, inflicting pain on those daring to doubt.

Medieval fat-cat clergy lived in comparative luxury while underprivileged citizens scrambled to survive. Crusaders, marching under religion's banner, drained wealth and destroyed lives in God's name.

The scientific visionary, Galileo, lived under house arrest for disputing church tradition.

His crime?

Suggesting, correctly, that the earth orbited the sun!

Less fortunate dissenters faced torture on racks intended to disarticulate bones, inducing "confessions" from victims to "save" their souls. Some "heretics," refusing to recant, were burned at the stake.

Religious tyranny, furious at memory of the courageous John Wycliffe for having translated the Bible into the English language to be accessible to public study, exhumed his body and burned his bones.

Many medieval observers, repulsed by corrupt conduct masquerading as religion, found an excuse to reject religious pretense and to shrug-off God as myth, an innocuous abstraction.

Honest believers risked being viewed as weak and naïve.

When deceived by counterfeit faith, where the truth about God has been garbled, humans may believe they are rejecting God when in reality they are turning their backs on a phony, disgraceful misrepresentation of God.

Evolution's attempt to wrap the science mantle around imaginary surmising sings from the same page as counterfeit religion. Its scenario portrays a cynical psychodrama that begins in some mysterious, *"warm little pond,"* and ends in the darkness of eternal death.

A secular "religion," committed to belief in an abstract, random series of accidents lacks credibility.

Evolution's shallow postulate articulates Asimov's *"nothingness."*

Reliance on mystical convergence of inorganic matter by "natural" forces to explain life's genesis, worships at the feet of superstition---the antithesis of science, a dark, pagan religion of the occult!

The miracle of life, originating accidentally, is less likely than the creation of an encyclopedia of information from a print shop explosion! This thin soup recipe for life's origin lacks the skimpiest credentials, offering instead, a starvation diet of unsubstantiated myth.

It envisions life without intelligent design, a jungle menagerie of life forms mindlessly competing for survival, destined for extinction, and ending in forever death. Hopelessly obsolete and irrelevant to our past, present, or future, evolution exudes toxicity! If correct, the world's future is past tense, bleak with the prognosis of eternal extinction.

© nito

Imagine if evolution's faux "science" represents actuality!

Here and now, by random chance, gone tomorrow, without a trace or forever future?

And eternal death, the reward of evil, triumphs?

And God doesn't exist?

Bright minds power through mists of the unknown, intellectually searching for clues to existence.

The Bible red flags honest thinkers to danger, offering answers that bypass academia overlay while penetrating to the soul of the human heart.

"There is a way that seemeth right unto a man, but the end thereof are the ways of death." [3]

If the Old and New Testaments are factually true, the miracle of a literal, seven-day creation week is real and mankind owns a future!

All humans play roles in the conflict between good and evil now raging center stage in the cosmic "Theater of the Universe."

The Creator of life authored science!

Science and religion coalesce in a meaningful big picture. Looking to God is the beginning of all wisdom relating to science and life on earth. Recognition of true science leads to reverently bowing knees to its Author.

Overwhelming evolution's bleak philosophy, Biblical faith worships the Author of science, the Supreme Being who created man in His own image and blazed the trail for victory over death.

"For since the creation of the world God's invisible qualities---His eternal power and divine nature---have been clearly seen, being understood from what has been made, so that men are without excuse. For although they knew God, they neither glorified Him as God nor gave thanks to Him, but their thinking became futile and their foolish hearts were darkened.

"Although they claimed to be wise, they became fools...

"They exchanged the truth of God for a lie, and worshiped and served created things rather than the Creator..." [4]

"You alone are the Lord. You made the heavens, even the highest heavens, and all their starry hosts, the earth and all that is on it, the seas and all that is in them. You give life to everything..." [5]

With Planet Earth occupying a mere miniscule blip on the cosmic landscape, human beings have been reminded of their pedestal status, created in God's image, since not even a sparrow *"...is forgotten by God."* [6]

The "Big Picture" perspective points to mankind's culpability in the decline and fall of perfection on planet earth. Unlike evolution's death-to-death narrative, lacking purpose or direction, the Bible presents opportunity for reconciliation with God, through His Son, Jesus Christ.

© Alan Collins, sculptor, Loma Linda University Medical Center

The Good Samaritan

Evil originated in the heart of the angel Lucifer, a created being. Vested with beauty and blessed with the power of choice, he abandoned his prestigious "light bearer" position, accusing God of tyranny. As Satan, the jealous adversary, he became infatuated with his own malignant pride.

The devil and his angels were banished from the presence of God and confined to earth to demonstrate the consequences of evil.

"And there was war in heaven. Michael and his angels fought against the dragon, and the dragon and his angels fought back. But he was not strong enough, and they lost their place in heaven.

"The great dragon was hurled down---that ancient serpent called the devil or Satan, who leads the whole world astray. He was hurled to the earth and his angels with him." [7]

The Creator could have suppressed the rebellion by destroying Lucifer and his followers, but had He done so, other created beings in the universe might be inclined to obey God from fear of consequences rather than from genuine love and worshipful respect.

Earth became a cosmic theater enabling the entire universe to observe God's love, fairness and justice in action. No human is a box-seat spectator.   Each is a center-stage performer, vested with a part to play.

"We have been made a spectacle to the whole universe, to angels as well as to men." [8]

Satan, the earth-bound adversary of all things good, determined to convince the first humans of God's alleged tyranny and to scar a perfect creation in order to showcase his power and to express his hatred for God. Intent on revenge, the adversary not only corrupted creation but inspired evolution's deceptive fraud, claiming life created itself accidentally.[9]

Except for access to the fruit of the Garden of Eden's "Tree of Knowledge," Adam and Eve lived without restraint in an idyllic environment, created for a life of happiness, sustained by open access to the "Tree of Life" that perpetuated human life without end.

Satan, the all-time con artist, deceived Adam and Eve by appealing to their egos, promising they would acquire the wisdom "unfairly" denied them by God. It all came crashing down when the first couple succumbed to the fabrication that willful disobedience would not lead to death.

Evicted from the Garden for failing a simple test of trust, the pair did not die immediately but denied further access to the "Tree of Life," the debilitating death process set in. The phony "wisdom" acquired proved nothing more than knowledge of the consequences of evil.

Exposed to the killer virus infecting the soul, Adam and Eve lived to endure the agony of death in their immediate family when an enraged Cain murdered his younger brother Abel. Cut off from face-to-face contact with the Creator's *"superior rationality,"* [10] all creation was exposed to deterioration.

Bleak consequences of disobedience and distrust of God included a curse where the soil would *"produce thorns and thistles"* and humans would *"return to the ground since from it you were taken."* [11]

"…You had commanded, and it was carried out in me, that the earth should bring forth briars and thorns for me, and that with heavy labor I should gain my bread." [12]

The end-time spiritual picture includes cunning deceptions reminiscent of Satan's misleading promise of "knowledge" that enticed Adam and Eve.

Just as the first human couple were corrupted by blatant falsehoods, sophisticated modern minds are vulnerable to seduction by *"the secret power of the lawless one… already at work"* and of the *"powerful delusion"* that advances *"the work of Satan displayed in all kinds of counterfeit miracles, signs, and wonders and every sort of evil that deceives."* [13]

Scripture warns of an end-time deception, where Satan will appear *"proclaiming himself to be God,"* [12] impersonating the Creator and counterfeiting Christ's return to earth. A dazzling figure, speaking pious platitudes, can deceive all but the most astute who look forward to Christ *"coming with clouds and every eye will see him."* [14]

The evil versus good spiritual drama reaches a showdown moment when the crucified Christ eventually returns to earth to award eternal life to all believers; to destroy evil for all time; and to make all things new!

"This same Jesus, who has been taken from you into heaven, will come back in the same way you have seen him go into heaven." [15]

Worshipped by millions, Christ's life revolutionized world history! The epic story of Christ's birth, death, resurrection and promised return to make all things new is inextricably linked to the creation week miracle.

His resurrection authenticated victory over death and guaranteed life eternal to all who trust His word. Rather than finite minds attempting to explain or prove miracles, it is enough to believe and follow because He said it. More than intellectual gymnastics debating abstract theories, it comes down to the big picture perception of the truth about God.

Each human confronts an either/or personal choice!
Every life's plan without God at the core of the equation,
suffers from terminal limitation as to purpose, scope and longevity.

Humans are vested with the power to reason and to choose a forever destiny. Contrasting worldviews offer a clear-cut, either/or choice.

The evolution/creation debate reaches beyond academic sparring over dueling dogmas.   One view postulates evolution's random chance odds that exhaust remote probabilities. The other embraces intelligent design created by the Author of science. There is nothingness in between but unplanned accident, an intellectual no-man's land.

Both options are faith-based.

It's a life or death decision!

Moral choice is not without cost!

"For the wages of sin is death, but the gift of God is eternal life in Christ Jesus our Lord." [16]

The Old Testament's Joshua challenged followers to discard *"the gods your forefathers worshipped beyond the River and in Egypt, and serve the Lord…*

"Choose for yourselves this day whom you will serve…

"As for me and my household, we will serve the Lord." [17]

Creation week combined with the birth, death, and resurrection of Christ, exemplifies the life-giving power of the Lord God Almighty that points the *"Way"* to a new and better life style! Consciously choosing, by faith, to connect to infinite power, opens the door to abundant living's rewarding adventure!

In the midst of a population overrun by cruel, military suppression, Christ's ministry featured miracles, capturing the attention of a subjugated people craving freedom from oppression.

The miracle of bringing Lazarus back to life, days after death, defied all finite norms. This evidence of power over life itself underscored Christ's authority to create all things!

Miracles warrant celebration--creation of original life on earth; the birth of a child; the guarantee of life eternal; and the transformation of a wicked person into a "born again" spiritual being.

God's power to create original life includes the power to redirect a depraved life from degradation into a spiritual being committed to unselfish goodness! Beyond cosmetic superficiality, the inner person enjoys the same recreation in Christ's image that transformed the career path of Paul.

"The Lord is gracious and compassionate, slow to anger and rich in love. The Lord is good to all; he has compassion on all He has made." [18]

"Who touched me?"

You, together with God, are the church!

Any person, allied with the Creator, constitutes a majority.

Champions of faith, from all eras of history, comprise a royal line of faithful believers, who have walked the earth from the beginning of time.

Look around!

Something more than charismatic attraction inspired champions of faith like Noah, Abraham, Daniel, Moses, Peter and John to put their lives on the line in commitment to the Creator.

God exposed Saul of Tarsus to the light that brightened Planet Earth on the first day of creation week, causing a revolution in his heart. Saul, the persecutor embraced that power, voluntarily taking on a new identity as Paul the Apostle.

Polycarp, second century Bishop of Smyrna, like Paul, suffered a martyr's death because he refused to deny Jesus and worship the Roman Caesar as God!

It is never too early or too late in life to select the role you choose in the big picture now playing in the cosmic theater. God provides the power. The choice is yours alone, unrelated to any other person or organization.

Intellectual comprehension of the truth about God and the creation miracle is worthy but can be worthless and self-deluding without accepting Christ's promise to recreate and renew your inner heart and soul.

The mystery of Godliness defies human comprehension. Getting acquainted with God and learning to walk in His footsteps involves a miraculous, spiritually maturing experience.

Degrading evil infects humans.

Knowledge alone, without commitment to complete, spiritual renewal, lacks substance. True religion is not mere philosophical whim conjectured by meandering, mortal minds, but a miraculous, inner revolution that turns lives about face, away from evil, moving in the direction of good.

Every person recognizes his or her shortfalls. Evil won't relinquish its grip on the strongest willed person that fails to voluntarily connect to the infinite power that built the universe and created life.

But once faith embraces the truth about God, life reverses course and moves upscale. The dividend of *"the peace of God, which passeth all understanding,"* [19] buoys hearts like a golden cloud floating on cool sunshine.

Regardless of a blemished lifetime of wallowing in evil's muck and mire, it is never too late to invite the Creator to revolutionize the inner person. However depraved, no human being lives beyond the reach of God's love.

The crucified thief, enduring his final moments of life on a cross next to Christ, accepted the gift of Christ's perfection blotting out his lifetime record of evil in exchange for the promise of life eternal.

No matter the debauchery, the Creator can recreate any human heart. Revolutionary, life-changing miracles happen every day. Walking in the Lord's footsteps, characters scarred with pride, hate, cunning and greed, are rebuilt by the Creator's empowering forgiveness and love.

© Chuck Nelson

Abundant Living

Each day's dawn offers a blank page with a door open wide to abundant living.

When you choose fellowship with Christ, doubt, discouragement and depression are banished, along with any sin-marred past record. Miraculous modification takes over any time a human heart, saturated in evil, surrenders to God's power.

Access to the power that created all things is available to everyone ---conditioned only on the individual's voluntary free choice built on trust, expressed in humble rhetoric!

"Create in me a pure heart, O God, and renew a steadfast spirit within me." [20]

Character building involves a lifetime project. The occasional good deed or misdeed is not the final test. Humans are judged by the direction taken, not by occasional stumbles.

Instinctively and without hesitations, humans step into water to save the life of a drowning child. There is no inner debate as to "should I" or "should I not." Similarly, the trend in the spiritual life of a Christian is in the direction of doing what's right instinctively, because it is right.

The most influential sermons are not preached from a pulpit but are lived on the street, in the office and in the home. Talk-the-talk verbiage lacks the impact and influence of walk-the-walk action.

Once looking to the Lord and headed in the right direction, you can be secure in the promise that any shortfall will be covered by God's grace and Christ's perfection.

But that first step in the right direction can appear intimidating---almost like climbing the Himalayas without conditioning, training or a backpack!

Human pride, feeding selfish egos, corrupts hearts. Children depend on parents for survival. Christ counseled, *"Unless you change and become like little children, you will never enter the kingdom of heaven."* [21]

Spiritual growth and survival climbing those symbolic Himalayas requires absolute dependency on the power and guidance of the Creator.

That first step requires looking in the mirror, recognizing and turning your back on what's ugly, and then putting it all on the line while praying, *"God, have mercy on me, a sinner."* [22]

Forgiving enemies who have *"trespassed against us"* may appear to be another tough pill to swallow---but it is key to the cure cleansing the inner person. Again, the Bible promises *"If we confess our sins, he is faithful and just and will forgive us our sins and purify us from all unrighteousness."* [23]

God's followers are invited to rest from physical labor one day each week to commemorate the miracle of creation, freedom from physical bondage and the *"new birth"* celebrating delivery from sin's shackles.

"Trust in the Lord with all your heart and lean not on your own understanding;; in all your ways acknowledge Him, and He will make your paths straight." [24]

"Praise be to the God and Father of our Lord Jesus Christ!

"In his great mercy he has given us new birth into a living hope through the resurrection of Jesus Christ from the dead, and into an inheritance that can never perish,

spoil or fade---kept in heaven for you, who through faith are shielded by God's power until the coming of the salvation that is ready to be revealed in the last time." [25]

More than the miracle of transforming power, the God of the universe exemplifies compassion, forgiveness, ultimate justice and limitless love so incomprehensible that He sacrificed His own Son to salvage sinners.

"For God so loved the world that He gave His one and only Son, that whoever believes in Him shall not perish but have eternal life." [26]

The presence of those who walk the *"straight paths"* and *"acknowledge Him"* will brighten the world's environment by reflecting the illuminating light that overwhelmed the shroud of darkness enveloping Planet Earth at the beginning of that first day of creation week.

"The power of one is exponential when linked to the power of The One." [27]

Late in the fourth century, Christian leader Aurelius Augustinus, (Augustine) expressed insight that resonates today.

Christ *"was mortal as men are mortal, but He was righteous as God is righteous; and because the reward of righteousness is life and peace, He could, with His righteousness, united with God, cancel the death of justified sinners...*

"That they might be saved through faith." [28]

"The Power, and the Glory, Forever...." [29]

Endnotes

Chapter I

1---Brian Thomas, "Fossilized Materials Must Be Young," *Acts & Facts,* June, 2009, 17.

2---Wagner, Dennis, "2009 Annual Report: The Key Darwin and Design Science News Stories of the Year," *Access Research Network,* December 30, 2009.

3----Charles Darwin, *The Origin of Species,* 638.

4---Luigi Cavalli-Sforza, *Genes, Peoples, and Languages* (New York: North Point Press, 2000) 61 as cited by Eric Lyons and Kyle Butt, *The Dinosaur Delusion* (Montgomery, Alabama: Apologetics Press, Inc., 2008) 156.

5--- Creationwiki.org, "Carbon-14 Dating," 7 November, 2008.

6---Robert H. Brown, and C. L. Webster, "The Upper Limit of C-14 Age," *Origins*, Volume 15, 1988, 39.

7---Leonard Brand, 262, referencing P.A.L. Giem, *Scientific Theology,* (Riverside, California: La Sierra University Press, 1997) 134-137.

8---John Baumgardner, with D. Russell Humphreys, Steven A. Austin,, and Andrew A. Snelling, "Measurable ^{14}C in Fossilized Organic Materials," *The Fifth International Conference on Creationism 2003*, 127; and reported in *Acts & Facts,* Vol. 32, No. 10, October 2003.

9---Ian T. Taylor, *In the Minds of Men.* Minneapolis, Minn.: TFE Publishing, 1991, 316.

10---Gunter Faure, *Principles of Isotope Geology* (Somerset, N.J.: John Wiley and Sons, Inc., 1986), 120, 121, 291; Copyright 1986, John Wiley & Sons, Inc. Reprinted by permission of John Wiley & Sons, Inc. as cited in Robert H. Brown letter to Warren L. Johns, October 22, 1995.

11---Richard Milton, *Shattering the Myths of Darwinism* (Rochester, Vermont:: Park Street Press, 1997) 53-55.

12---Robert H. Brown letter to Warren L. Johns, 26 November 2003.

13---Michael A. Cremo and Richard L. Thompson, *Forbidden Archeology* (Los Angeles: Bhaktivedanta Book Publishing, Inc., 1996) 694.

14---Andrew A. Snelling, "The Cause of Anomalous Potassium-Argon 'Ages' for Recent Andesite Flows at Mt. Ngauruhoe, New Zealand, and the Implications for Potassium-Argon Dating," *ICC Symposium Sessions* (Pittsburgh: Creation Science Fellowship, Inc., 1998) 510; *The Fifth International Conference onCreationism* (Pittsburgh: Creation Science Fellowship, Inc., 2003) 285-303.

15---Andrew A. Snelling, "Radioisotope Dating of Grand Canyon Rocks: Another Devastating Failure for Long-Age Geology," *Institute for Creation Research,* 2010.

16---Barry Yeoman, "Sweitzer's Dangerous Discovery," *Discover*, Vol. 27, No. 4, April, 2006, 37.

17---Brian Thomas citing V. Morel, "Dino DNA: the Hunt and the Hype. *Science*. 261 (5118): 160.

18---Unveil the "Holy Grail" of Paleontology in *Secrets of the Dinosaur Mummy*. Discovery Channel. Posted on discovery.com, accessed April 2, 2009, cited by Brian Thomas, "Fossilized Materials Must Be Young," *Acts & Facts,* June, 2009, 17.

19---Brian Thomas, citing D. Criswell, "How Soon Will Jurrasic Park Open? *Acts & Facts*. 35 (6).

20---"Dinosaur Mummy," *National Geographic News*, June 30, 2009.

21---Jason Palmer, "Dinosaur Mummy Yields Its Secrets," *BBC News,* June 30, 2009.

22---Charles Q. Choi, "Cache in Chinese Mountain Reveals 20,000 Prehistoric Fossils," *LifeScience.com,* December 22, 2010.

23---R.L. Wysong, *The Creation-Evolution Controversy*. (East Lansing, Michigan: Inquiry Press, 1976) 348.

Chapter II

1---Denyse O'Leary, "One of the many Thomas Edisons you didn't know about," ARN Announce, Access Research Network, February 14, 2011.

2---*Holy Bible,* New International Version (Grand Rapids, Michigan, Zondervan Bible Publishers. 1978, Genesis 1:3.

3---___________, Genesis 1:2.

4---___________, Mathew 5: 14, 16.

5---___________, Genesis 1:14.

6--- *Holy Bible,* New International Version, Genesis 1:16.

7---This data is from an unidentified internet source. While believed to be true, its accuracy has not been verified independently.

8---Eric Lyons and Kyle Butt, *The Dinosaur Delusion* (Montgomery, Alabama: Apologetic Press, Inc., 2008) 202.

9---*Holy Bible,* New International Version, Genesis 1:2.

10---__________, 1 Timothy 3:16.

11---__________, Deuteronomy 5:15

12---David Person, "150 Years Later, Civil War Redux," USA *Today,* 2-23-2011.

13---Stephen Budiansky, "Terror in the South," *Secrets of the Civil War* (U.S. News and World Report, 2008) 80.

14---See Brian Bull, Fritz Guy & Ervin Taylor, Editors, *Understanding Genesiss,* (Riverside, CA, Adventist Today, 2006).

15---*Holy Bible,* King James Version, Mark 2: 27.

16---*Holy Bible*, New International Version, Deuteronomy 4:20.

Chapter III

1---Michael Denton, *Evolution: A Theory in Crises* (Bethesda, Maryland: Adler & Adler, 1986) 358.

2---John Morris & Steven A. Austin, *Footprints in the Ash,* (Green Forest, Arkansas: Master Books, 2003) 67. See also, Steven A. Austin, "Excess Argon with Mineral Concentrations From the New Dacite Lava Dome at Mount St. Helens Volcano," *Creation Ex Nihilo Technical Journal* 10 (1996), part 3; cited by *Acts and Facts,* Institute for Creation Research (May,1997) 26:5.

3---*The Holy Bible,* New International Version, Genesis 1:2.

4---Mark Swarts, "Scientists Confirm Age of the Oldest Meteorite Collision on Earth," *SpaceDaily.com*, August 23, 2002.

5---*The Holy Bible*, King James Version, Job 38:7.

6---Robert H. Brown letter to Warren L. Johns, 26 November 2003.

7---Frank Lewis Marsh, "On Creation with an Appearance of Age," *Creation Research Society Quarterly,* 1978, 14[4] 187, 188 as cited by Bert Thompson, *Creation Compromises* (Montgomery, Alabama: Apologetics Press, 2000) 270.

8---This summary is based upon the eyewitness account of Dr. Harold G. Coffin, paleontologist, who walked Surtsey, July, 1967.

9---*The Holy Bible,* New International Version, Hebrews 1:1, 2.

10---See Charles H. Hapgood, *Maps of the Ancient Sea Kings* (Kempton, Illinois: Adventures Unlimited Press, 1996) Preface, 193-197 & 244.

11---*Stephen B. Cox, "Atlantean-Egyptian Library," http:espah.tripod.com/europeanlibrary,* retrieved from internet, January 24, 2011.

12---*The Holy Bible,* New International Version, Genesis 11:3-7.

13---Eric Lyons, "Moses and the Art of Writing," ApologeticsPress.org/articles/779, March, 2010.

14---Samuel Wang and Ethel R. Nelson, *God and the Ancient Chinese* (Dunlap,Tennessee: Read Books, 1998) 31.

15---Geoffrey Barraclough, *TheTimes Atlas of World History* (London: Times Books Limited, 1978) 40, 52.

16---See *Smithsonian*, November, 2008, feature, Gobekli Tepe, Turkey.

17---See "Fossils in Antarctica," *British Antarctica Survey*, www.antarctica.ac.

Chapter IV

1---*The Holy Bible*, New International Version, Romans 8:22.

2---*Wikipedia,* "Antikythera Mechanism," retrieved from internet January 22, 2011.

3---John Anthony West, *The Serpent in the Sky,* (New York, NY: Harper and Row, 1984) as cited by David Hatcher Childress, *Technology of the Gods,* (Kempton, Illinois: Adventures Unlimited Press, 2000) 12.

4---Charles Darwin to Asa Gray, cited by Adrian Desmond and James Moore, *Darwin,* (New York: W.W. Norton and Company, 1991) *477.*

5---Yuri N. Ivanov, "Laws of Fertility, Role of Natural Selection, and Destructiveness of Mutations." *Creation Research Society Quarterly*, Vol. 17, December, 2000, 157.

6--Duane Arthur Schmidt, *And God Created Darwin* (Fairfax, Virginia: Allegiance Press, 2001) 131.

7---D. S. Allen and J. B. Delair, *Cataclysm* (Santa Fe, N. M.: Bear & Co., 1997) 107.

8--John Yeld, "Fossil Tracks of Giant Scorpion a World First," *Independent Online 2002*, August 29, 2002.

9---Elizabeth Kolvwer, "The Sixth Extinction?", *The New Yorker,* May 25, 2009, 57.

10---*Creation*, 24(2):54, March-May, 2002.

11---See Ronald Pickering, *Nature Science Update*, 30 January 2002, online report Info@CreationResearch.net, February 14, 2002.

12--Dennis R. Peterson, *Unlocking the Mysteries of Creation* (El Dorado, California: Creation Resource Publications, 2002) 28.

13---Ariel A. Roth, *Origins.* (Hagerstown, Md.: Review and Herald Publishing Association, 1998) 182.

14---William Jacobs, "Goliath Squid by the Side of the Road," *Discover,* May, 2003, 16.

15---*Nature Science Update*, April 30, 2002.

16---*The Holy Bible*, New International Version, Genesis 6:4.

17---__________, Numbers 13:32-33.

18---For a detailed discussion see www.secondlaw.com/two.

19---Granville Sewell, "Evolution and the Second Law of Thermodynamics," www.isic.org/boards/ubb-get_topic-f-10-t-000038, January, 2004. Dr. Sewell serves in the Mathematics Department of Texas A&M University. Serious scholars deserve a look at Dr. Sewell's examination of evolution theory in the context of the second law of thermodynamics.

20---*Holy Bible*, New International Version, Genesis 3:4.

21---__________,Psalms 106:25, 26.

Chapter V

1---Alfred Russell Wallace, *Darwinism* (London and New York, Macmillan and Co., 1890) 379, 380.

2---*The Holy Bible*, New International Version, Genesis 7:17-24.

3---*The Holy Bible,* King James Version, Genesis 1:2.

4---Mark Shwartz, "Scientists Confirm Age of the Oldest Meteorite Collision on Earth," *News Service*, (650) 723-9296; mshwarts@stanford.edu, August 20, 2002.

5---Gretel Schueller, "Australia's Ups and Downs," Earth (August 1998) 16.

6---Wilbur A. Nelson, *The Scopes Trial* (Birmingham, Ala.: The Legal Classics Library, 1984) a reprint of *The World's Most Famous Trial* (Cincinnati: National Book Co., 1925) 238-241.

7---Charles Darwin, *Origin of Species*, 648.

8---Richard Milton, *Shattering the Myths of Darwinism* (Rochester, Vermont: Park Street Press, 1997) 77, 78.

9---"Mystery of the Megaflood," Nova, 2005, pbs.org/previews/Nova_Megaflood.

10--Tom Vail, *The Grand Canyon: A Different View* (Green Forest, Arkansas: Master Books, 2003) 9.

11---Leonard Brand, *Faith, Reason, and Earth History.* Berrien Springs, Mich.: Andrews University Press, 1997) 254, 255.

12---Richard Milton, *Shattering the Myths of Darwinism* (Rochester, Vermont: Park Street

13---*The Holy Bible,* New International Version, Genesis 7:11, 19, and 20.

14---__________, Genesis 8:1.

15--__________, Genesis 6: 5-11

16---__________, Genesis 9:13, 16.

17---Lyall Watson, "The Water People," *Science Digest*, 90[5]:44, May, as cited by Eric Lyons and Kyle Butt, *The Dinosaur Delusion*, (Montgomery, Alabama: Apologetics Press, Inc., 2008) 140.

18---*The Holy Bible,* New International Version, Genesis 9:16.

Chapter VI

1---John C. Whitcomb and Henry M. Morris, *The Genesis Flood* (Phillipsburg, New Jersey: Presbyterian and Reformed Publishing Company, 1995) 203.

2---Charles Q. Choi, "Cache in Chinese Mountain Reveals 20,000 Prehistoric Fossils," *LifeScience.com,* December 22, 2010.

3---Kathy Sawyer, "New Light on a Mysterious Epoch," *The Washington Post* (February 5, 1998).

4---Richard Milton, *Shattering the Myths of Darwinism*, 92.

5---__________, *Shattering the Myths of Darwinism*, 93.

6---Lyall Watson, "The Water People," *Science Digest*, 90[5]:44, May, as cited by Eric Lyons and Kyle Butt, *The Dinosaur Delusion*, (Montgomery, Alabama: Apologetics Press, Inc., 2008) 140.

7---Gretel Schueller, "Earth News: Death in the Dunes," *Earth* (June 1998) 11.

8---Luis Chiappe, "Dinosaur Embryos," *National Geographic* (December 1998) 38.

9---Ida Thompson, *National Audubon Society Field Guide to North American Fossils* (New York: Alfred A. Knopf, Inc., 1994) 765.

10--- Scott M. Huse, *The Collapse of Evolution* (Grand Rapids, Michigan: Baker, 1997) 96. A 1910 Geological Survey of Canada pictured a polystrate tree protruding vertically through multiple layers of sedimentary rock. (See photo, Ian T. Taylor, *In the Minds of Men* (Minneapolis: TFE Publishing, 1996) 114.

11---See Trevor Major, *Genesis & the Origin of Coal* (Montgomery, Alabama: Apologetics Press, 1996).

12--- John Paulien, *Armageddon at the Door* (Hagerstown, Maryland: Autumn House Publishing, 2008) 13.

13---See *The Washington Post Weekly Edition*, June 13-19, 2005, 10.

14---See Michael Guillen, *Five Equations that Changed the World*, 210.

15---David E. Shormann, "Novarupta and the Valley of 10,000 Smokes: Begging for a Biblical Interpretation," *Creation Research Society Quarterly,* Spring, 2010, 249.

16---Joel Achenbach, "When Yellowstone Explodes," *National Geographic,* August, 2009, 60, 61.

17---Larry Vardiman, "Are Hurricanes Getting More Destructive?", *Impact #390* (El Cajon, California: Institute for Creation Research, December, 2005) iv, referencing his previous research, L. Vardiman, 1996, *Sea-Floor Sediment and the Age of the Earth,* ICR Technical Monograph, Institute for Creation Research, EI Cajon, CA, 94 pp. and L. Vardiman., 2001, *Climates before and after the Genesis Flood: Numerical Models and Their Implications,* ICR Technical Monograph, Institute for Creation Research, EI Cajon, CA, 110 pp.

18---Michael J. Oard, *An Ice Age Caused by the Genesis Flood* (El Cajon, California: Institute for Creation Research, 1990) 33.

19---Michael J. Oard, *An Ice Age Caused by the Genesis Flood* (El Cajon, California: Institute for Creation Research, 1990) 34.

20---Tom Canby, "The Year Without a Summer," *Legacy* (Sandy Spring, Maryland: Sandy Spring Museum, 2002) Winter Edition.

21---Larry Vardiman, "Greenland Ice Cores," *CreationDigest.com.*, Winter, 2002; an updated version of "Impact Article #226" published by *The Institute forCreation Research* , April, 1992.

22---Margaret Olds, *Geologica* (New South Wales, Australia: Millennium House Pty Ltd., 2007) 402-3.

23---Dan Vergano, "Greenland Glacier Runoff Doubles Over Past Decade," *USA Today*, February 17, 2006, 24.

24---Rob Crilly, "Remote Somali Village Reels from Latest Hardship," *USA Today*, January 7, 2005, 5A.

25---See Chris Hawley, 'Researchers Explore Mysteries Surrounding 65-million-year-old Crater," *USA Today*, March 2, 2005, 9D.

Chapter VII

1---See Colin Patterson lecture, "Can You Tell Me Anything About Evolution," as transcribed by Wayne Frair and reported in "Bridge to Nowhere," *Creation Digest.com* website, Autumn 2004 Edition. Patterson, a lifelong evolutionist researcher, shared these and other doubts in an 1981 lecture before an audience of scientists at New York's American Museum of Natural History.

2-- Henry Gee, *In Search of Deep Time* (New York: The Free Press, 1999) 116, 117.

3---See *"Ida Fossil Discovery,"* The Darwinian Masillae, www.AgeoftheSage.org.

4---Randolph E. Schmid, "Before Lucy Came Ardi, New Earliest Hominid Found," *Yahoo News*, October 1, 2009.

5---Ann Gibbons, "Breakthrough of the Year, *Ardipithecus ramidus*," *Science*, December 18, 2009, Vol. 326, 1598-99.

6---Roddy M. Bullock, "Darwinists on Design: Jumping to Confusions," citing 1860 Darwin letter to Asa Gray, a designist, *The ID Report*, www.Discover.org, February 28, 2009.

7---Charles Darwin, *The Descent of Man,* Vol. II, 389.

8---___________, *Descent,* Vol. I, 203.

9---___________, *Descent,* Vol. II, 386.

10---___________, *Descent,* Vol. II, 389, 390.

11---___________, *Descent,* Vol. I, 207.

12---___________, Descent, Vol. II, 389.

13---___________, *Descent,* Vol. I, 206.

14---___________, Letter to Asa Gray, cited by Adrian Desmond and James Moore, *Darwin,* (New York: W.W. Norton and Company, 1991) 456.

15---___________, *Descent,* Vol. II, 328

16---___________, *Descent,* Vol. II, 327.

17---___________, *Descent,* Vol. I, 169.

18---___________, *Descent,* Vol. I, 168

19---___________, *Descent,* Vol. II, 216.

20---___________, *Descent,*, Vol. I, 201.

21---___________, *Descent,* Vol. I, 213.

22---___________, *Descent,* Vol. I, 173.

23---David Person, "150 years later; Civil War Redux," *USA Today,* February 23, 2011.

24---___________, Descent, Vol. 1, 213.

25---See Jamie Shreeve, "From Africa to Astoria by Way of Everywhere," *National Geographic*, September, 2009, 24.

26---*Creation Matters* (Vol. 15, No. 6, November/December, 2010) 7, citing Carnegie Museum of Natural History (2010, October 28, "Into Africa? Fossils Suggest Earliest Anthropoids Colonized Africa," *Science Daily*.

27---___________, citing R. Kaufman, "Oldest Modern Human Outside of Africa Found," *National Geographic News*, October 25, 2010.

28---"'Out of Africa' Theory Boost: Skull Dating Suggests Modern Humans Evolved in Africa," *Science Daily*, January 12, 2007.

29---See Richard M. Cornelius's definitive summary of the trial , "Scopes Trial: The Trial Gavel Heard Round the World," (*CreationDigest.com*, Winter, 2006) as excerpted from *Impact* (Dayton, Tennessee: Bryan College, 2000) v-xiii.

30---Fay Cooper-Cole, *The Scopes Trial* (Birmingham, Ala.: The Legal Classics Library, 1984) 237; a reprint of *The World's Most Famous Trial* [Cincinnati: National Book Co., 1925], 238-241.

31---George H. Hunter, *Civic Biology* (1914) 195, 196.

32---Lane P. Lester and Raymond G. Bohlin, *The Natural Limits to Biological Change* (Dallas: Probe Books, 1989) 54.

33---See *National Geographic*, "BODY: The Complete Human."

34---This list of the remarkable functions of the human organism is from the internet, author unknown. The veracity is presumed but is not authenticated.

35---See *The American Heritage Dictionary of the English Language,* some say thenumber exceeds 500,000).

36---*The Holy Bible,* King James Version, Genesis 8:4, 5. Clearly, angels were supernatural beings, created a little higher than *Homo sapiens.* Could secular speculative preoccupation with "aliens" inadvertently imply reference to angels of the Bible?

37---*The Holy Bible,* New International Version, Hebrews 13:2.

38---See "Mitochondrial Eve," Wikepedia.org referencing D.L Rohde, S. Olson and J.T. Chang, "Modeling the Recent Common Ancestry of All Living Humans," *Nature* (September, 2004) 431 and D.L. Rohde, "On the Common Ancestors of All Living Humans," submitted to *American Journal of Anthropology*, 2005.

Chapter VIII

1---Carolyn Leaf, *Who Switched Off My Brain?* (Southlake, TX: Inprov, 2009) 23.

2---See Dennis Normile, "Gene Expression Differs in Human and Chimp Brains," *Science*, 6 April 2001, 44, 45, presented at "Genes and Minds Initiative Workshop on Ape Genomics" in Tokyo, March 14-15, 2001.

3---See Duane T. Gish, *Evolution: The Fossils Still Say No!* (El Cajon, Calif.: Institute for Creation Research, 1995), 19, 20; Michael Denton, *Evolution: A Theory in Crisis* (Bethesda, Md.: Adler & Adler, 1986) 330, 331; and Harold Coffin with Robert H. Brown, *Origin by Design* (Hagerstown, Md.: Review and Herald Publishing Assn., 1983) 382.

4---Michael Denton, *Evolution: A Theory in Crisis* (Bethesda, Md.: Adler & Adler, 1986) 330.

5---C.P. Yu, "The Human Brain Testifies Against Evolution: Confessions of a

Neurosurgeon," (Internet Website: www.hkam.org.hk/temp/counterevolution, as noted 1-10-2005).

6---Harold Coffin with Robert H. Brown, *Origin by Design* (Hagerstown, Md.: Review and Herald Publishing Association, 1983) 383.

7---Sharon Begley, "I can't Think," *Newsweek*, March 7, 2011, with apartial quote from Sheena Iyengar, *The Art of Choosing*.

8---*The Holy Bible*, King James Version, Proverbs 23:7.

9--- Carolyn Leaf, *Who Switched Off My Brain?* (Southlake, TX: Inprov, 2009) 20.

10---__________, *Who Switched Off My Brain?* (Southlake, TX: Inprov, 2009) 29.

11---________, *Who Switched Off My Brain?* (Southlake, TX: Inprov, 2009) 109.

12---*The Holy Bible*, New International Version, Luke 23d:34.

13---__________, 1 John 1:9.

14---*The Holy Bible*, New International Version, Ephesians 4:31, 32.

15---*The Holy Bible,* New International Version, John 10:10.

16--Charles Darwin to T. Huxley, June 2, 1859, Desmond & Moore, *Darwin*, 475.

17---Adrian Desmond & James Moore, *Darwin*, (New York: W.W. Norton and Company, 1991) 477.

18---*The Holy Bible*, New International Version. Acts 17:24-26,

Chapter IX

1---Wernher von Braun, as quoted by James Perloff, *Tornado in a Junkyard,* (Arlington, Massachusetts: Refuge Books, 1999) 253.

2---William B. Provine, Cornell University Professor of Biological Sciences summarizing "naturalistic evolution" in a 1998 Darwin Day keynote address, as per Sean Pittman's www.DetectingDesign.com.

3---See *National Geographic*, "Killer Stress" video.

4---Wernher von Braun, as quote by James Perloff, *Tornado in a Junkyard,* (Arlington, Massachusetts: Refuge Books, 1999) 253.

5---Ian T. Taylor, "The Idea of Progress," *The Fifth International Conference on Creationism,* (Pittsburgh: Creation Science Fellowship, Inc., 2003) 578.

6---*The Holy Bible,* New International Version,, Hebrews 12:1.

7---___________, Acts 7:60.

8---__________, Acts 8:3.

9---__________, Acts 9:1-18.

10---__________, 2 Thessalonians 2:3, 4.

11---An insightful observation, author unknown.

Chapter X

1---George Frideric Handel, *The Messiah* (1741-42).

2---*The Holy Bible, King James Version,* John 14:6.

3---*The Holy Bible,* New International Version, John 18:38.

4---*The Holy Bible,* King James Version, Mathew 5:3-10

4---*The Holy* Bible, New International Version, Mathew 5:14 & 15.

Chapter XI

1---Rick Warren, "Starbucks Stirs Things Up with a God Quote on Cups," *USA Today*, October 19, 2005, 8D.

2---*The Holy Bible,* New International Version, II Timothy 3:5.

3---__________, Proverbs 14:12.

4---__________, Romans 1:20-25.

5---__________, Nehemiah 9:6.

6---__________, Luke 12:6.

7--_*The Holy Bible*, New International Version, Revelation 12:7-9. These words of John the disciple and the revelator deserve credence. John walked at the side of Christ, an eyewitness to His life, death and resurrection. He devoted his own life to the founding of the Christian church and penned messages he learned from Christ's ministry.

8---__________, I Corinthians 4:9.

9---Could it be that a gene-mutating virus is a parasite genetically engineered by Satan, the adversary of all things good? More than choosing to defy God by tasting forbidden fruit, did Adam and Eve bite into parasite poison? While such an idea is only speculative, the Genesis account of the emergence of rampaging evil is genuine. Depraved humans became capable of murder and the ground shared the curse by producing *"thorns and thistles."*

10---Wernher von Braun, as quoted by James Perloff, *Tornado in a Junkyard,* (Arlington, Massachusetts: Refuge Books, 1999) 253.

11---*The Holy Bible,* New International Version, Genesis 3:19.

12---Aurelius Augustinus, *Confessions,* written between 397-398 AD, references Genesis 3:18, 19, Albert C. Outlew's translation, revised by Mark Vessey (New York, Barnes and Noble, 2007) 55.

13---*The Holy Bible,* New International Version, 2 Thessalonians 2:3-13.

14---___________, Revelation 1:7.

15---___________, Acts 1:11.

16---*The Holy* Bible, King James Version, Romans 6:23.

17---*The Holy Bible,* New International Version, Joshua 24:14, 15.

18---___________, Psalms 145:8, 9.

19---*The Holy* Bible, King James Version, Philippians 4:7.

20---*The Holy Bible,* New International Version, Psalms 51:10.

21---___________, *Matthew* 18:3.

22---___________, Luke 18:13.

23---___________, I John 1:9.

24---___________, Proverbs 3:5, 6.

25---___________, I Peter 1:3-5.

26---___________, John 3:16.

27---Marilynn Peeke, "From the Pulpit," *Visitor*, October, 2009, 5.

28---Augustinus, Aurelius (Augustine), *Confessions,* written between 397-398 AD, Albert C. Outlew's translation, revised by Mark Vessey (New York, Barnes and Noble, 2007). circa 397 AD, 183.

29---*The Holy* Bible, King James Version, Mathew 6:9-13.

The Miracle of Life's Beginning

The Holy Bible's sixty-six books were written by inspired writers over a period of fifteen hundred years. More than a mere compilation of ancient history and rules for better living, the Bible addresses life's classic questions of where we came from, what we are doing here and where we are going.

Central to the basic "Big Picture" theme is the story of the life, death, and resurrection of Christ, our Creator and God's *"only begotten"* Son.

Moses, beneficiary of ancient Egypt's sophisticated education reserved for royalty, is credited with having written the Genesis account of Creation. John the Beloved, walked by Christ's side during His ministry, witnessed His crucifixion, and penned the gospel of Johns and the prophetic Book of Revelation.

Perceptions of Moses, Daniel, David, Peter, Mathew, John and Paul, flow as complimentary parts of a contiguous whole. Taken together, the Old and New Testaments of the Bible provide direction, meaning, and purpose for every human life.

The story of the Bible's authorship, preservation, and compilation depicts a miracle. Collectively, manuscripts *Codex Sinaiticus, Codex Vaticanus,* and *Codex Alexandrinus* authenticate the Scripture narrative with its incomparable perspective of ancient human history.

Thanks to Augustine, Bishop of Hippo, and other fourth-century Christians, the complete Scriptural canon was assembled formally---nearly two centuries before Gregory, Bishop of Rome (590-604 A.D.) assumed the full religious and civil power of the Papacy. The Latin Vulgate Bible published by Johannes Gutenberg in 1450-55 used the canon approved by the Synod of Hippo, 393 A.D.

Bible built faith, and science, are not in conflict but mutually supportive. The Creator of all things is the Author of true science.

Evolution, Darwin style, never happened! The theory is faux science and a dark philosophy. It starts in unknown blackness and ends in forever death.

© Warren L. Johns

The quest for discovering the truth about God
and the miracle of His creation starts
with prayerful study of the Bible.

Achenbach, Joel, "When Yellowstone Explodes," *National Geographic,* August, 2009.

___________, "The Origin of Life Through Chemistry," *National Geographic,* March, 2006, 31.

Adams, Leslie B., Jr., Editor/Publisher, *The Scopes Trial* Birmingham, Alabama: The Legal Classics Library, 1984; a reprint of *The World's Most Famous Trial* (Third Edition) Cincinnati: National Book Company, 1925.

Age-of-the-Sage.org, "The Darwinius masillae."

Allan, D. S., and J. B. Delair. *Cataclysm.* Santa Fe, N.M.: Bea & Company, 1997.

Alter, Jonathan, "The President's 'Whiz Kids'", *Newsweek,* June 1, 2009.

American Heritage Dictionary of the English Language, The, Third Edition, New York: Houghton Mifflin Co., 1992.

Appenzeller, Tim. "The Genes of 1996." *Discover,* January, 1997.

___________. "Test Tube Evolution Catches Time in a Bottle, "*Science* 284, June 25, 1999.

Army's Edgewood Chemical Biological Center at Aberdeen Proving Grounds, Maryland, www.plosone.org/home.action, **October 7, 2010.**

Asp, Karen, "Rocks of Ages," *USA Today Open Air,* Spring, 2009.

Augustinus, Aurelius (Augustine), *Confessions,* **written between 397-398 AD, Albert C.Outlew's translation, revised by Mark Vessey (New York, Barnes and Noble, 2007).**

Austin, Steven A. "Excess Argon With Mineral Concentrates From the New Dacite Lava Dome at Mount St. Helens Volcano." *Creation Ex Nihilo Technical Journal,* vol. 10, part 3, 1996; as reported in "Acts and Facts," *Institute for Creation Research,* May, 1997.

___________, Editor. *Grand Canyon: Monument to Catastrophe,* .Santee, Calif.: Institute for Creation Research, 1994.

___________, "Interpreting Strata of Grand Canyon," in Austin, *Grand Canyon: Monument to Catastrophe,* Santee, California: Institute for Creation Research. 1994.

___________, "*Nautiloid Mass Kill and Burial Event, Redwell Limestone, Grand Canyon* Region," *Pittsburgh: International Conference on Creationism, 2003.*

Barinaga, Marcia, "Tracking Down Mutations That Can Stop the Heart," *Science* 281, July 3, 1998.

Barraclough, Geoffrey, *The Times Atlas of World History ,* London: Times Books Ltd, 1978.

Baumgardner, John with D. Russell Humphreys, Steven A. Austin,, and Andrew A.Snelling, "Measurable ^{14}C in Fossilized Organic Materials," *The Fifth International Conference on Creationism 2003*, 127; *Acts & Facts*, Vol. 32, No. 10, October 2003.

Begley, Sharon, "I can't Think," *Newsweek*, March 7, 2011, with apartial quote from Sheena Iyengar, *The Art of Choosing.*

Bird, W.R., *The Origin of Species Revisited*, Vol. I , Nashville: Regency, 1991.

Bradley, Walter L. and Charles B. Thaxton, "Information and the Origin of Life," in *The Creation Hypothesis*, ed. J.P. Moreland, Downers Grove, Illinois: Inter Varsity Press, 1994.

Brand, Leonard. *Faith, Reason, and Earth History*. Berrien Springs, Mich.: Andrews University Press, 1997.

Brown, David, "Limits to Genetic Evolution," *The Washington Post*, July 7, 2003.

__________, "Scientists Discover 3 More Genes With Links to Alzheimer's Disease," *The Washington Post*, September 7, 2009, A3.

Brown, Robert H., "Amino Acid Dating," *Origins*, 1985, 12-8-25.

__________, *Letter to Warren L. Johns*, 26 November, 2003.

Brown, Robert H, and C.L. Webster, "Interpretation of Radiocarbon and Amino Acid Data," Origins, 1991.

__________,"The Upper Limit of C-14 Dating," *Origins*, Volume 15, 1988.

Budd, Graham E. & Maximillian J. Telford, "Evolution: Along Came a Sea Spider," *Nature*, Vol. 437, October 20, 2005, as cited by Frank Sherwin, "Un-Bee-lievable Vision," *Acts & Facts* (El Cajon, California: ICR, Vol. 35, No. 2, February, 2006.

Budiansky, Stephen, "Terror in the South," *Secrets of the Civil War* (*U.S. News and World Report*, 2008) 80.

Buettner, Dan, *The Blue Zones,*(Washington, D.C., National Geographic, 2009.)

Bull, Brian, Fritz Guy & Ervin Taylor, Editors, *Understanding Genesiss,* (Riverside, CA, Adventist Today, 2006).

Bullock, Roddy M., "Darwinists on Design: Jumping to Confusions," citing 1860 Darwin letter to Asa Gray, a designist, *The ID Report*, www.Discover.org, February 28, 2009.

Canby, Tom, "The Year Without a Summer," *Legacy*, Sandy Spring, Maryland: Sandy Spring Museum, 2002, Winter Edition.

Cavalli-Sforza, Luigi, *Genes, Peoples, and Languages,* New York: North Point Press, 2000.

Chiappe, Luis, "Dinosaur Embryos," *National Geographic*, December 1998.

Childress, David H., *Technology of the Gods,* (Kempton, Illinois: *Adventures* Unlimited Press,2000).

Choi, Charles Q., "Cache in Chinese Mountain Reveals 20,000 Prehistoric Fossils, *LiveScience.com*, December 22, 2010.

Coffin, Harold G., description of walk on beach, Surtsey, July, 1967.

Coffin, Harold, with Robert H. Brown, *Origin by Design*. Hagerstown, Md.: Review and Herald Publishing Association, 1983.

Creation, 24(2):54, March-May, 2002.

Creation Matters **(Vol. 15, No. 6, November/December, 2010).**

Creationwiki.org, "Carbon-14 Dating," 7 November, 2008.

Cremo, Michael A., and Richard L. Thompson. *Forbidden Archaeology*. Los Angeles: Bhaktivedanta Book Publishing, Inc., 1996.

Crilly, Rob, "Remote Somali Village Reels from Latest Hardship," *USA Today*, January 7, 2005.

Darwin, Charles Robert, *On the Origin of Species by Means of Natural Selection, or the Preservation of Favored Races in the Struggle for Life*, First Edition facsimile, 1859, Cambridge: Harvard University Press.

__________, *The Origin of Species* (Sixth Edition), New York: Random House, Inc., 1993.

__________, *The Descent of Man, and Selection in Relation to Sex*, Vol. I & Vol. II Princeton, N.J., Princeton University Press, 1981.

__________, Letter to Asa Gray, cited by Adrian Desmond andJames Moore, *Darwin*, New York: W.W. Norton and Company, 1991.

__________, Letter to J.D. Hooker [1 February] 1871, in Darwin, F., ed., *The Life and Letters of Charles Darwin*, [1898], New York: Basic Books, Vol. II, 1959.

__________, (1881) in Darwin, F., *The Life and Letters of Charles Darwin,* London: John Murray, 1888, Vl. 3, cited by Michael Denton, *Evolution: A Theory in* Crisis.

Davies, Paul, *The Cosmic Blueprint: New Discoveries in Nature's Ability to Order the Universe,* New York: Simon & Schuster, 1988.

__________, *The Mind of God*, New York: Simon & Schuster, 1992.

Declaration of Independence, United States of America, July 4, 1776.

Demick, David A., "The Blind Gunman," *Impact* (El Cajon, Calif.: Institute for Creation Research, February, 1999) iv.

Desmond, Adrian & James Moore, *Darwin*. New York, Warner Books, Inc., 1991.

Denton, Michael, *Evolution: A Theory in Crisis*. Bethesda, Md.: Adler & Adler, 1986.

__________, "An Interview with Michael Denton," Access Research Network, Origins Research Archives, Vol. 15, Number 2, July 20, 1995.

Dawson, Sir William, *The Story of Earth and Man* (New York: Harper and Brothers, 1887).

Faure, Gunter, *Principles of Isotope Geology.* Somerset, N.J.: John Wiley and Sons, Inc., 1986.

Friend, Tim, "Gene Defect is Linked to Parkinson's," *USA Today*, June 27, 1997, and *USA Today*, January 17, 2005.

Gee, Henry, *In Search of Deep Time: Beyond the Fossil Record to a New History of Life*, New York: The Free Press, 1999.

Gibbons, Ann, "Breakthrough of the Year, *Ardipithecus ramidus*," *Science*, December 18, 2009, Vol. 326.

Gish, Duane T., *Evolution: The Fossils Still Say No!* El Cajon, Calif.: Institute for Creation Research, 1995.

__________, *Creation Scientists Answer Their Critics.* El Cajon, Calif.: Institute for Creation Research, 1993.

Gitt, Werner, *In the Beginning was Information*, Green Forest, Arkansas: Master Books, 2006.

__________, "Carbon-14 Content of Fossil Carbon," *Origins*, Number 51, 2001.

Glausiusz, Josie. "Fast Forward Aging." Discover, November, 1996.

__________. "The Genes of 1996." *Discover*, January 1997.

Gould, Stephen Jay, *The Panda's Thumb*, New York: W.W. Norton, 1980.

__________, "The Return of Hopeful Monsters, "*Natural History*, 86[4]:22-30, June-July, 1977.

__________, Speech at Hobart College, February 14, 1980, cited by Luther Sunderland, *Darwin's Enigma*, El Cajon, California: Master Books, 1984 cited by Bert Thompson and Brad Harrub, "*National Geographic* Shoots Itself in the Foot Again," Apologetics Press.Org online report, 2004.

Greene, Brian, as quoted by Carl Warner, *Living Fossils, Evolution: the Grand Experiment,* Green Forest, AR: New Leaf Press, 2008.

Guillen, Michael, *Five Equations that Changed the World,* New York: Hyperion, 1995.

Gupta, Sanjay, *CNN Health,* "Girl's mother just had "feeling Something Was Wrong," 9-21-2010).

Hapgood, Charles H. *Maps of the Ancient Sea Kings* (Kempton, Illinois: Adventures Unlimited Press, 1996).

Harrub, Brad and Bert Thompson, "Creationists Fight Back: A Review of *U.S. News & World Report's* Cover Story On Evolution," Montgomery, Alabama: Apologetics Press,2002.

Hawley, Chris, "Researchers Explore Mysteries Surrounding 65-million- year-old Crater," *USA Today*, March 2, 2005.

Handel, George Frideric, *The Messiah* **(1741-42).**

Holy Bible, King James Version, New York: Oxford University Press; also New International Version, Grand Rapids: Zondervan Bible Publishers, 1978.

Hoyle, Sir Fred, "The Big Bang in Astronomy," *New Scientist*, November 19, 1981.

__________, *The Universe: Past and Present Reflections.* Cardiff: University College,1981.

Hoyle, Sir Fred and Chandra Wickramasinghe, *Evolution from Space,* London: J.M. Dent & Sons, 1981.

Hubbard, Ruth and Elijah Wald, *Exploding the Gene Myth*, Boston: Beacon Press1997, citing Francis Galton, *Inquiries Into Human Faculty,* London: Macmillan, 1883.

Humphreys, D. Russell Ph.D. with **John R. Baumgardner, Ph.D., Steven A. Austin, Ph.D.,** and **Andrew A. Snelling, Ph.D.,** "Helium Diffusion Rates Support Accelerated Nuclear Decay," *The Fifth International Conference on Creationism*, Robert L. Ivey, Jr., Editor, Pittsburgh: Creation Science Fellowship, 2003.

Hunter, Cornelius G., *Darwin's Proof*, Grand Rapids, Michigan: Brazos Press, 2003.

Huse, Scott M., *The Collapse of Evolution*, Grand Rapids, Michigan: Baker, 1997.

Huxley, Sir Julian, *Evolution After Darwin* ed. Sol Tax, vol. 3, Chicago: University of Chicago Press, 1960, the Centennial Celebration of the *Origin of Species.*

Internet, www.beyondbooks.com. "Bacteria and Viruses."

Internet, http://en.wikipedia.org/wikl/Epigenetics.

Ivanov, Yuri N., "Laws of Fertility, Role of Natural Selection, and Destructiveness of Mutations." *Creation Research Society Quarterly*, Vol. 17, December, 2000

Jacobs, William, *"Goliath Squid by the Side of the Road,"* Discover, *May, 2003.*

Jastrow, Robert, *Until the Sun Dies,* New York, W.W. Norton, 1977, as quoted by Bert Thompson, *The Scientific Case for Creation.*

Johns, Warren LeRoi. *Ride to Glory*, Brookeville, Maryland: General Title, Inc., 1999.

__________, *Beyond Forever*, Smithville, Tennessee: *Creation Digest, 2007.*

__________, *Genesis File*, Smithville, Tennessee, www.GenesisFile.clom, 2010.

Kemp, T.S.,, *Fossils and Evolution, Oxford University, Oxford University Press, 1999.*

Keosian, John, In Haruhiko Nada, ed., *Origin of Life*, Tokyo: Center for Academic Publications, Japan Scientific Publications Press, 1978.

King, Colbert I., "A Dangerous Kind of Hate," *The Washington Post*, September12, 3009.

Kilbert, Elizabeth, "The Sixth Extinction?", *The New Yorker,* May 25, 2009.

Leaf, Caroline, *Who Switched Off My Brain?* (Southlake, TX, InProcv, 2009).

Lester, Lane P., and **Raymond G. Bohlin.** *The Natural Limits to Biological Change* Dallas, Texas: Probe Books, 1989.

Lipka, Mitch,*Consumer Ally,* "Meat Tainted With Deadly Virus is Being Sold to Consumers," September 28, 2010

Løvtrup, Søren. *The Refutation of a Myth,* New York: Croom Helm, 1987.

Lubenow, Marvin L., *Bones of Contention.* Grand Rapids, Michigan: Baker Books,1992, 2004.

Lyons, Eric and Kyle Butt, *The Dinosaur Delusion,* Montgomery, Alabama: Apologetic Press, 2008.

Mackay, John, "Evidence News Update No. 4, *Creation Research*, April 2, 2003.

Major, Trevor, *Problems in Radiometric Dating,* Research Article Series, Montgomery, Alabama: Apologetics Press, Inc., undated publication.

Marsh, Frank Lewis. "On Creation with an Appearance of Age," *Creation Research Society Quarterly,* 1978, 14[4].

McElheny, Victor K. *Watson and DNA,* Cambridge, Massachusetts: Perseus Publishing, 2003.

Milton, Richard. *Shattering the Myths of Darwinism.* Rochester, Vermont.: Park Street Press, 1997.

Morris, John & **Steven Austin**, *Footprints in the Ash,* Green Forest, Arkansas: Master Books, 2003.

Morowitz, Harold J., *Energy Flow in Biology,* New York: Academic Press, 1968.

Murray, Michael J., *Reason for the Hope Within,*Grand Rapids, Michigan: Eerdmans, 1999.

National Geographic, November, 1999; and promo, "BODY: The Complete Human."

National Geographic News, "Dinosaur Mummy," June 30, 2009.

Nature Science Update, April 30, 2002.

Nelson, Wilbur A., *The Scopes Trial* , Birmingham, Ala.: The Legal Classics Library, 1984.

Normile, Dennis, "Gene Expression Differs in Human and Chimp Brains," *Science*, 6 April 2001, presented at "Genes and Minds Initiative Workshop on Ape Genomics" in Tokyo, March 14-15, 2001.

Nova, "Mystery of the Megaflood," pbs.org/previews/Nova_Megaflood., Nova, 2005,

Oard, Michael J., "The Origin of the Grand Canyon, Part II, Fatal Problems with the Dam-Breach Hypothesis," *Creation Research Society Quarterly,* Spring, 2010, 290.

__________, *An Ice Age Caused by the Genesis Flood* El Cajon, California: Institute for Creation Research, 1990.

Olasky, Marvin and John Perry, *Monkey Business,* Nashville: Broadman & Holman, Publishers, 2005.

Olds, Margaret, *Geologica,* New South Wales, Australia: Millennium House Pty Ltd., 2007.

Overman, Dean L., *A Case Against Accident and Self-Organization.* New York: Rowman & Littlefield Publisher, Inc., 1997.

Palmer, Jason, "Dinosaur Mummy Yields Its Secrets," *BBC News,* June 30, 2009.

Patterson, Colin, "Can You Tell be Anything About Evolution," lecture as transcribed by Dr. Wayne Frair and reported in "Bridge to Nowhere?", *CreationDigest.com,* Autumn 2004 Edition.

Paulien, John, *Armageddon at the Door* , Hagerstown, Maryland: *Autumn House Publishing, 2008.*

Peeke, Marilynn, "From the Pulpit," *Visitor,* October, 2009.

Person, David, "150 Years Later, Civil War Redux," USA *Today,* 2-23-2011.

Peterson, Dennis R. *Unlocking the Mysteries of Creation* (El Dorado, California: Creation Resource Publications, 2002) 28.

Pennisi, Elizabeth. "Genome Data Shakes Tree of Life." *Science* 280, May 1, 1998.

__________, "New Gene Found for Inherited Macular Degeneration." *Science* 281, July 3, 1998.

Perloff, James. *Tornado in a Junkyard,* Arlington, Mass.: Refuge Books, 1999.

Pickering Ronald, *Nature Science Update,* 30 January 2002, online report Info@CreationResearch.net, February 14, 2002.

Provine, William B., 1998 Darwin Day keynote address, as reference by Sean Pittman in his website, www.DetectingDesign.com.

Rappuoli, Rino, Henry L. Miller, and **Stanley Falkow,** "The Intangible Value of Vaccination," *Science* Vol. 297, 9 August 2002.

Rees, Martin and **Priyamvada Natarajan,** "Invisible Universe," *Discover,* December, 2003.

Roth, Ariel A. *Origins.* Hagerstown, Md.: Review and Herald Publishing Assn., 1998.

Ruse, Michael, *The Evolution-Creation Struggle* , Cambridge: Harvard University Press, 2005.

Ryan, William and **Walter Pitman,** *Noah's Flood.* New York: Simon & Schuster, 1998.

Sawyer, Kathy. "New Light on a Mysterious Epoch," *The Washington Post,* February 5, 1998.

Schmidt, Duane Arthur, *And God Created Darwin* (Fairfax, Virginia: Allegiance Press, 2001).

Scmid, Randolph E., "Before Lucy Came Ardi," *Yahoo News,* October 1, 2009.

Science, Vol. 295, 25, 11 Jan 2002.

Science Daily, January 12, 2007 "'Out of Africa' Theory Boost: Skull Dating Suggests Modern Humans Evolved in Africa."

Schueller, Gretel. "Australia's Ups and Downs." *Earth,* August, 1998.

__________, "Earth News: Death in the Dunes," *Earth,* June, 1998.

Siebert, Charles, "Unintelligent Design," *Discover*, March, 2006.

Sewell, Granville, "Evolution and the Second Law of Thermodynamics," www.isic.org, January, 2004.

Shelton, J. S., *Geology Illustrated* , San Francisco and London:W. H. Freeman and Co.

Shormann, David E., "Novarupta and the Valley of 10,000 Smokes: Begging for a Biblical Interpretation," *Creation Research Society Quarterly,* Spring, 2010, 249.

Shreeve, Jamie, "From Africa to Astoria by Way of Everywhere," *National Geographic*, September, 2009, 24.

Shwartz, Mark, "Scientists Confirm Age of the Oldest Meteorite Collision on Earth," *News Service*, (650) 723-9296; mshwarts@stanford.edu, August 20, 2002.

Smith, Shelton, "What We Believe," *www.SwordoftheLord.com.*

Snelling, Andrew A., "The Cause of Anomalous Potassium-Argon 'Ages' for Recent Andesite Flows at Mt. Ngauruhoe, New Zealand, and the Implications for Potassium-Argon Dating." *ICC Technical Symposium Sessions*, Robert E.Walsh, Editor.Pittsburgh: Creation Science Fellowship, Inc. 1998.

__________, "Radioisotope Dating of Grand Canyon Rocks: Another Devastating Failure for Long-Age Geology," *Institute for Creation Research,* 2010.

Star, The, Ventura, California, June 24, 1997.

Steel , Karen P. and Steve D. M. Brown, "More Deafness Genes." *Science* 280, May 29, 1998.

Stein, Rob, "Sex May Rid Us of DNA Flaws," *The Washington Post* ,February 1, 1999, A9.

Sunderland, Luther, *Darwin's Enigma: Fossils and Other Problems*, San Diego: Master Books, 1988.

Taylor, Ian T. *In the Minds of Men*. Minneapolis, Minn.: TFE Publishing, 1991.

__________, "The Ultimate Hoax: Archaeopteryx Lithographica," *Proceedings of the Second International Conference on Creationism, Vol.. II* , Pittsburgh: Creation Science Fellowship, Inc., 1990.

__________, **"The Idea of Progress,"** *The Fifth International Conference on Creationism*, Pittsburgh Creation Science Fellowship, Inc., 2003.

Thomas, Brian, "Fossilized Materials Must Be Young," *Acts & Facts,* June, 2009.

__________, citing D. Criswell, "How Soon Will Jurrasic Park Open? *Acts & Facts*. 35.

__________, "Fossilized Materials Must Be Young," *Acts & Facts,* June, 2009.

Thaxton, Charles B., Walter L. Bradley and **Roger L. Olsen,** *The Mystery of Life's Origin*, New York: Philosophical Library, 1984.

Thompson, Bert, *The Scientific Case for Creation*, Montgomery, Alabama: Apologetic Press, Inc., 2002.
__________,*The Scientific Case for Creation* ,Montgomery, Alabama: Apologetics Press, 2002.

Thompson, Ida. *National Audubon Society Field Guide to NorthAmerican Fossils*. New York: Alfred A. Knopf, Inc., 1982.

USA Today, Editorial Page, " 'Intelligent Design' Smacks of Creation by Another Name," August 9, 2005.

Vail, Tom, *Grand Canyon: A Different View*. Green Forest, Arkansas: Master Books, 003.

Vardiman, Larry, "Are Hurricanes Getting More Destructive?", *Impact #390* El Cajon, California: Institute for Creation Research, December, 2005) iv.

__________, "Greenland Ice Cores," *CreationDigest.com.*, Winter, 2002.

Vardiman, Larry, Andrew A. Snelling and **Eugene F. Chaffin,** Editors, *Radioisotopes and the Age of the Earth*, Vol. 1, 2000 and Vol. II, 2005, published jointly by Institute or Creation Research, E Cajon, California and Creation Research Society, Chino Valley, Arizona.

Vergano, Dan, "Soil Points to Comet Storm That Was Fatal to Mammoth," *USA Today*, January 2, 2009.

__________, "Greenland Glacier Runoff Doubles Over Past Decade," *USA Today*, February 17, 2006.

Von Braun, Wernher, as quote by James Perloff, *Tornado in a Junkyard,* Arlington, Massachusetts: Refuge Books, 1999.

Wallace, Alfred Russell. *The Geographical Distribution of Animals, With a Study of the Relations of the Living and Extinct Faunas as Elucidating Past Changes of the Earth's Surface*. New York: Harper, 1876.

__________, *Darwinism*, London and New York, Macmillan and Co., 1890.

__________, "The Present Position of Darwinism," *Contemporary Review*, August, 1908.

Wang, Samuel and **Ethel R. Nelson** *God and the Ancient Chinese*. Dunlap, Tennessee: Read Books Publisher, 1998.

Warren, Rick, *The Purpose Driven Life,* Grand Rapids, Michigan: Zondervan, 2002.

__________, "Starbucks Stirs Things Up with a God Quote on Cups," *USA Today*, October 19, 2005.

Wachtershauser, Gunter, Letter to Editor, *Science*, 25 October 2002, vol. 298.

Wang, Samuel and Ethel R. Nelson, *God and the Ancient Chinese,* Dunlap, Tennessee: Read Books, 1998.

Washington Post, The, "Genetic Error Causes Rapid-Aging Syndrome,"April 17, 2003.

__________, *Weekly Edition,* **June 13-19, 2005.**

Watson, Lyall, "The Water People," *Science Digest*, 90[5]:44, May, as cited by Eric Lyons and Kyle Butt, *The Dinosaur Delusion*, Montgomery, Alabama: Apologetics Press, Inc., 2008.

Weaver, Daniel C.,"The River of Life," *Discover,* November 1997.

Weiss, Rick. "Defect Tied to Doubling of Risk for Colon Cancer." *The Washington Post*, August 26, 1997.

__________, "Water Scarcity Prompts Scientists to Look Down," *Washington Post*, March10, 2003.

Wells, Spencer, "From Africa to Astoria by Way of Everywhere," Genographic Project, *National Geographic,* September, 2009.

West, John Anthony, *The Serpent in the Sky* (New York, NY: Harper and Row, 1984).

Whitcomb ,John C. and **Henry M. Morris,** *The Genesis Flood,* Phillipsburg, New Jersey: Presbyterian and Reformed Publishing Company, 1995.

Wickramasinghe, Chandra, "Threats on Life of Controversial Astronomer," *New Scientist,* January 21, 1982.

Will, George F. "The Gospel of Science." *Newsweek,* November 9, 1998.

Wise, Kurt P., *Faith, Form and Time*, Nashville: Broadman & Holman, Pubs., 2002.

Witham, Larry A., *Where Darwin Meets the Bible.* New York: Oxford University Press, 2002.

Wikedia.org, "Mitochondrial Eve," citing Rohde, DL, Olson, S, Chang, JT, "Modeling the Recent Common Ancestry of all Living Humans," *Nature,* (September, 2004).

Wysong, Randy L., *The Creation-Evolution Controversy*East Lansing, Michigan: Inquiry Press, 1976.

Yeld, John ,"Fossil Tracks of Giant Scorpion a World First," *Independent Online 2002,* August 29, 2002.

Yeoman, Barry, "Schweitzer's Dangerous Discovery," *Discover,* April, 2006.

Yockey, Hubert P., *Information Theory and Molecular Biology.* Cambridge: Cambridge University Press, 1992.

Yu, C.P. "The Human Brain Testifies Against Evolution: Confessions of a Neurosurgeon," Internet Website: www.hkam.org.hk/temp/counterevolution, as noted 1-10-200

Ozymandius References

Wikipedia, Shelley, Percy Bysshe (1819). *Rosalind and Helen, a modern eclogue, with other poems.* London: C. and J. Ollier. OCLC 1940490. and Shelley, Percy Bysshe (1826). *Miscellaneous and posthumous poems of Percy Bysshe Shelley.* London: W. Benbow. OCLC 13349932. The texts are identical except spelling "desert" or "desart."

Studio Six, May 18, 2006

Author
Warren LeRoi Johns (1929-)

Born the year of the arrival of commercial airline services, the first ever Academy Awards presentation, and the onset of the Great Depression, Johns practiced law as a career in California, Maryland, and the District of Columbia until partial retirement in the summer of 1992.

Admitted to practice before the United States Supreme Court in 1963, he has been a member of the American Association for the Advancement of Science. His 1999 *Ride to Glory* targeted some of evolution's more obvious shortfalls while a lawyer's academic perspective documented evolution's most obvious *"flaws"* and *"holes."* This was followed by his 2007 *Beyond Forever; Genesis File* in 2009, and 2011's *Chasing Infinity.*

Earlier his non-fiction *Dateline Sunday, U.S.A.,* drew national attention as a legal history documenting blue law confrontation with the U.S. Constitution's first amendment.

A 1958 graduate of the University of Southern California's Law Center, and holder of La Sierra University's 1994 "Alumnus of the Year" award, the author's professional resume appears in *Who's Who in American Law, Who's Who in America,* and *Who's Who in the World.*

Warren L. Johns, Esq. (ret.)
wj1935@yahoo.com

"…The fool says in his heart, 'There is no God.' "
Psalms 14:1

CPSIA information can be obtained
at www.ICGtesting.com
Printed in the USA
237755LV00005BA